PRACTICAL READING 2

- Recreation and Hobbies
- Good Cooking
- Behind the Wheel
- It's the Law!

READING in context

READING *in context*

PRACTICAL READING 1
PRACTICAL READING 2
READING NONFICTION 1
READING NONFICTION 2
READING FICTION 1
READING FICTION 2

SADDLEBACK PUBLISHING·INC.

Three Watson
Irvine, CA 92618-2767

Website: www.sdlback.com

Development and Production: Laurel Associates, Inc.
Cover Design: Elisa Ligon
Interior Illustrations: Ginger Slonaker

ISBN 1-56254-190-0

Printed in the United States of America
05   9 8 7 6 5 4 3 2 1

CONTENTS

A NOTE TO THE STUDENT

Skillful readers have many advantages in life. While they are in school, they obviously get better grades. But the benefits go far beyond the classroom. Good readers are also good thinkers, problem-solvers, and decision-makers. They can avoid many of the problems and frustrations that unskilled readers miss out on. In short, good readers have a much greater chance to be happy and successful in all areas of their lives.

READING IN CONTEXT is an all-around skill-building program. Its purpose is to help you achieve your goals in life by making you a better reader. Each of the six worktexts has been designed with your needs and interests in mind. The reading selections are engaging and informative—some lighthearted and humorous, others quite serious and thought-provoking. The follow-up exercises teach the essential skills and concepts that lead to reading mastery.

We suggest that you thumb through the book before you begin work. Read the table of contents. Notice that each of the four units is based on a unifying theme. Then take a moment to look through the four lessons that make up each theme-based unit. Scan one of the *Before reading* paragraphs that introduces a lesson. Glance at the *Preview* and *Review* pages that begin and end each unit. "Surveying" this book (or any book) in this informal way is called *prereading*. It helps you "get a fix on" the task ahead by showing you how the book is organized. Recognizing patterns is an important thinking skill in itself. And in this case it will make you more comfortable and confident as you begin your work.

Happy reading!

RECREATION AND HOBBIES

LESSON 1: Collecting Stamps

LESSON 2: Fishing Guide

LESSON 3: Community Centers

LESSON 4: Cycling

When you complete this unit, you will be able to answer questions like these:

- *How little could you spend for a stamp that is 125 years old?*

- *What kind of lures are good for catching striped bass?*

- *Where could you look for listings of upcoming recreational events in your community?*

- *What's the difference between a mountain bike and a hybrid bike?*

PRETEST

Write **T** or **F** to show whether you think each statement is *true* or *false*.

1. _____ Stamps with printing errors are worth more than stamps that are perfectly printed.

2. _____ Touring bikes are especially designed for commuters who carry heavy backpacks.

3. _____ Ticket prices may be high for events that are held to benefit a worthy cause.

4. _____ The first U.S. postage stamps went on sale more than 200 years ago.

5. _____ The "grandfather" of the modern bicycle was called a *cyclotron*.

6. _____ Local museums usually have reduced rates for children and senior citizens.

Pretest answers: 1. T 2. T 3. T 4. F 5. F 6. T

COLLECTING STAMPS

Before reading. . .

Do you know a philatelist? Are *you* one, by any chance? Stamp collecting is one of the most popular collecting hobbies in the world. It has been called "the king of hobbies and the hobby of kings." Students of stamps are called *philatelists*. The name comes from two Greek words—*philos*, meaning "love," and *stelos*, meaning "paid." Stamps are signs that the postage has been paid.

FAMOUS "FIRSTS"

May 6, 1840: Great Britain issues the first stamps to prepay postage on letters. The first stamp cost one penny and is now known as the "Penny Black."

July 1, 1847: America's first postage stamps go on sale. One stamp, which costs five cents, features a portrait of Benjamin Franklin, the first Postmaster General. The 10-cent stamp issued at the same time pictures George Washington, Revolutionary War hero and the first U.S. president.

THE HISTORY OF STAMP COLLECTING

No one knows exactly when stamp collecting started. It probably occurred right after the first stamp was issued. We do know that the first stamp catalog was published in 1864. Since then, stamp catalogs have been published in almost every country.

People soon discovered that some stamps were harder to find than others. Why? Because smaller quantities were printed. Finding these rarer stamps became a challenge to early collectors. They soon began to trade rare stamps and sell them to each other. Prices were low in the beginning. But as more and more people collected stamps, prices began to go up.

Then some stamps with printing errors first appeared. Perhaps the center illustration was printed upside down. Perhaps the wrong kind of paper or ink was used. Since such errors were usually very rare, these stamps became greatly valued. Soon, well-developed collections of rare stamps became important investments—as valuable as collections of fine art jewelry.

DIFFERENCES IN STAMPS

Many stamps look the same to a beginning collector. But to a philatelist, small differences in stamps mean a great deal. What do they look for? Things such as the paper and inks used, the way the stamps are separated, the printing process, and the postal history.

THE VOCABULARY OF STAMPS

Stamps are available in *used* or *mint* condition. A used stamp has actually been used for postage. The stamp will bear a cancellation mark, and the gum will be missing from the back. A mint stamp is in good, uncanceled condition.

The first stamps weren't easy to separate. Post office clerks and stamp users had to cut them apart. These stamps are said to be *imperforate*. Modern stamps have rows of small holes that allow them to be separated quickly and easily. These holes, or *perforations*, were developed in 1847.

Watermarks are faint patterns impressed into paper when it is manufactured. To discourage counterfeiting, the U.S. once used a watermark consisting of the letters *USPS*. Today, watermarks are no longer used on U.S. stamps.

Stamps that honor important people, places, and events are called *commemoratives*. These special stamps are usually larger and more colorful than regular stamps. They are printed in limited quantities and sold only for a limited time.

Regular stamps—the kind most often used on everyday mail—are called *definitives*. These are the "workhorses" of the stamp world. They are often reprinted over a period of several years. This time span results in subtle differences between stamps that at first appear to be the same.

Times Square 2000 Station
December 31 1999
New York NY 10036

Happy New Year!
Official Commemorative Cachet

WHY PEOPLE COLLECT STAMPS

Not all people collect stamps because they are rare or special. Many collectors simply enjoy the pictures of out-of-the-way places and things. Some people collect stamps from one country only. Others collect only stamps showing birds or ships or railroads. Still others collect stamps of only one color, such as purple stamps. Specialists may collect just one issue—or varieties of one issue. Your reasons for collecting stamps don't matter, as long as you are having fun!

- Stamps are history you can hold in your hand. They can take you wherever you want to go in the past—from the American Revolution to the Wild West and into outer space.

- "Armchair travelers" can satisfy their wanderlust by collecting stamps from all around the world.

- Getting started doesn't cost much. For about 75 cents, you can buy a canceled U.S. stamp that is more than 125 years old.

COMPREHENSION

Write **T** or **F** if the statement is *true* or *false*. Write **NI** if there is *no information* in the reading to help you make a judgment.

1. _____ The British Guiana one-penny stamp of 1856 is the largest stamp in the world.

2. _____ Stamps are kept in glassine envelopes until they are mounted in an album.

3. _____ The word *philatelist*, meaning stamp collector, was formed by combining two Greek words.

4. _____ Very small differences in stamps can make a very big difference in how much they are worth.

5. _____ In the United States, stamps were sold for the first time in the middle of the 18th century.

6. _____ *Commemorative* stamps are sold only for a limited time period.

7. _____ A stamp in *mint* condition is worth more than a used stamp.

8. _____ London, England, is the stamp-collecting capital of the world.

SYLLABLES

Divide the words from the reading into syllables (the separate sounds in a word).

revolutionary	perforation	philatelist	commemorative

1. _____ / _____ / _____ / _____

2. _____ / _____ / _____ / _____

3. _____ / _____ / _____ / _____ / _____

4. _____ / _____ / _____ / _____ / _____ / _____

PUZZLER

Use words from the reading to solve the crossword puzzle. Answers are words that complete the sentences.

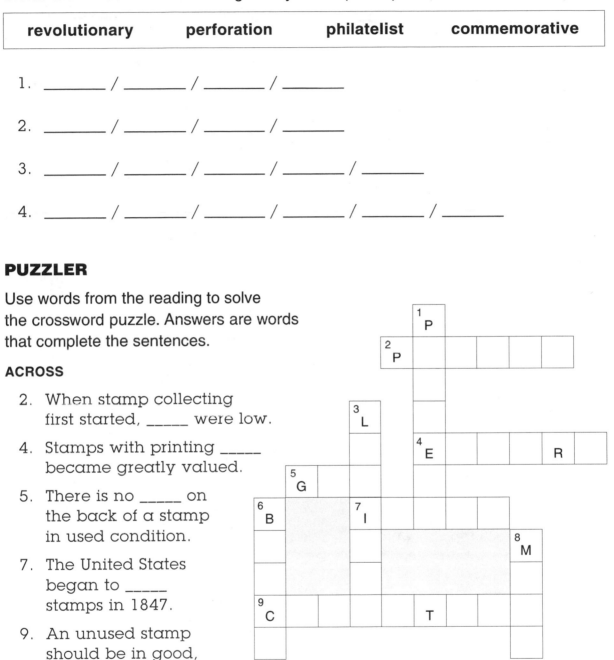

ACROSS

2. When stamp collecting first started, _____ were low.

4. Stamps with printing _____ became greatly valued.

5. There is no _____ on the back of a stamp in used condition.

7. The United States began to _____ stamps in 1847.

9. An unused stamp should be in good, uncanceled _____.

DOWN

1. Mistakes are sometimes made in the printing _____.

3. Commemorative stamps are printed in _____ quantities.

6. The first stamp ever printed is now known as the "Penny _____."

8. A perfect stamp that has never been used is said to be in _____ condition.

COMPOUND WORDS

Make compound words to complete the sentences. Use one word from Box A and one word from Box B to make the compounds. Hint: You will *not* use all the words in the boxes.

BOX A		
path	trail	up
down	water	every
stage	some	work

BOX B		
mark	spots	finder
side	day	horses
shows	horses	coach

1. The _____ once used on U.S. stamps consisted of the letters *USPS*.

2. Stamps called *definitives* are the _____ of the stamp world.

3. America's largest stamp is the Mars _____.

4. In rare cases, the illustration on a stamp might be printed _____ down.

5. One triangular stamp bears a picture of a _____.

6. Stamps regularly used for _____ mail are reprinted over a period of several years.

SPELLING

Circle the correctly spelled word in each group.

1.	2.	3.	4.
feachur	separate	valubel	regyaler
feature	seperate	valuble	reguler
feeture	sepperate	valuable	regaler
featchure	seperete	valueble	regular

VOCABULARY

Circle a letter to show the meaning of the **boldface** word.

1. **Subtle** differences in stamps are of great interest to collectors.

   a. having subtitles
   b. having fine distinctions
   c. having obvious errors

2. Collecting stamps can satisfy the **wanderlust** of "armchair travelers."

    a. tendency to   b. sense of awe   c. yearning for
        go astray   and wonder   travel

3. The United States once used a watermark on stamps to discourage **counterfeiting**.

    a. overcrowding at   b. manufacture   c. stamps with counter-
        post office counters   of fake stamps   clockwise designs

4. Watermarks are **impressed** into the paper when it is manufactured.

    a. pressed down   b. favorably   c. printed with
        with some force   influenced   black letters

5. Well-developed stamp collections are important **investments**.

    a. contributions to   b. investigations   c. use of money
        the post office   of history   to gain a profit

SENTENCE COMPLETION

First, unscramble the words from the reading. Then use the words to complete the sentences.

TAIRTROP _____	**GATESOP** _____
DRETA _____	**ROFREEMTIPA** _____
SAGEMI _____	**STILIPCASES** _____

1. _____ stamps cannot easily be separated.

2. A stamp on an envelope is a sign that _____ has been paid.

3. Some stamp collectors are _____ who collect only one issue.

4. Benjamin Franklin's _____ is on America's first five-cent stamp.

5. The Mars Pathfinder stamp has hidden _____ that can be detected only with a decoder lens.

6. Early collectors soon began to _____ rare stamps.

FISHING GUIDE

Before reading. . .

Fishing has always been a favorite activity in America. Few other forms of recreation provide sport, enjoyment of nature—and perhaps a delicious dinner! Watch your local newspaper for a Fishing Guide like this one.

RIVERS AND STREAMS

◆ **LOWER SACRAMENTO (SACRAMENTO AREA):** The hot catch along the entire river is shad, with most from two to five pounds. Fishing for stripers, most eight to 12 pounds, is good for bait anglers. Trollers catch stripers in clear water with Broken Back Rebels. Bass fishing is good in Folsom Lake with fairly large bass in the trees. Anglers report bass are hitting on plastics from the surface down to 15 feet. Salmon up to four pounds are caught with Goldeneyes, Mooselook, and Uncle Larry's Lures. For salmon and trout, troll in the 30- to 40-foot range.

BAY & DELTA

◆ **HOT PICK:** Isleton, San Pablo Bay stripers

◆ **ISLETON:** Fishing has improved since Mother's Day weekend with reports of stripers at the Isleton and Rio Vista bridges and at Steamboat Slough. Female trout in the 15- to 20-pound range are caught with grass shrimp and salted sardines. Cooler weather this weekend will also help. Some sturgeon in the six- to 10-pound range were reported in the Pittsburg area.

◆ **SUISUN:** Spotty fishing this past week, but some sturgeon were caught near the Mothball Fleet. A few stripers and catfish were biting.

◆ **SAN PABLO BAY:** Good fishing for stripers and halibut at The Brothers, Red Rock, Angel Island, and Southampton by drifting shiners. Stripers, most six to 10 pounds with some up to 18, are caught along with halibut in the five- to 10-pound range. Try fishing on the anchor in the Pumphouse area with shrimp baits in 10 to 15 feet of water.

OCEAN

◆ **HOT PICK:** Half Moon Bay salmon

◆ **HALF MOON BAY:** Salmon fishing is excellent and anglers have caught early limits of fish, most six to 20 pounds, throughout the week. The best areas have been seven to 10 miles off the deep reef and eight miles south of the coast. Anglers take half-limits of rockfish. Fishing for rock cod is improving, but not many lingcods have been caught.

◆ **SANTA CRUZ:** Salmon fishing has been slow with boats taking about a half-fish per rod off Moss Landing in Monterey. Slow fishing for stripers, halibut, and rock cod. Fishing for rock cod is expected to improve. A couple of white sea bass have been caught. Five lingcods from six to 12½ pounds were caught this past week.

LAKES

◆ **HOT PICK:** San Pablo trout

◆ **SAN PABLO:** Anglers report limits of trout after a 3,600-pound load was stocked this week. Use PowerBait or a night crawler and marshmallow combination. The water has cleared since the rain, and trolling has improved. Use chartreuse or fire-tiger colors.

◆ **PARKWAY:** Trout fishing is good for anglers using PowerBait or night crawlers at the south bank, back cove, and either side of the peninsula. The next trout plant is scheduled for Friday. Sturgeon fishing is fair. Use shrimp baits or night crawlers at the tip of the peninsula or the south bank. Catfish season is over until the summer.

COMPREHENSION

Write **T** or **F** if the statement is *true* or *false*. Write **NI** if there is *no information* in the Fishing Guide to help you make a judgment.

1. _____ This guide comments on local fishing conditions within the last month.

2. _____ Parkway is a narrow, rushing stream in the mountains.

3. _____ Salmon fishing has been slow in Santa Cruz.

4. _____ Long Island is the best place to go if you want to catch rock cod.

5. _____ Salmon recently caught in Half Moon Bay range from six
to 20 pounds.

6. _____ Because of pollution, there are fewer fish in the bay than
there used to be.

LOCATING INFORMATION

Complete the sentences. Find the information you need in the Fishing Guide.

1. Parkway Lake will be stocked with trout on _____.

2. On fishing boats in _____, the catch averages
one-half fish per rod.

3. Shad is currently the hot catch in the Sacramento
_____.

4. Cooler weather this weekend will improve fishing at
_____.

5. _____ fishing has recently been good at
Folsom Lake.

WORD COMPLETION

Add vowels (a, e, i, o, u) to complete the names of some of the fish
mentioned in the Fishing Guide.

1. A S H __ N __ R is a freshwater minnow often used as bait.

2. A H __ L __ B __ T is an edible flatfish; some weigh hundreds
of pounds.

3. The flesh of a S___LM___N is yellowish pink or pale red when cooked.

4. TR___ ___T are food and game fish that are usually spotted.

5. L___NGC___D are large game fish found in the North Pacific.

6. A ST___RG___ ___N is a large, primitive food fish with a projecting snout.

NOTING DETAILS

Use information in the Fishing Guide to answer the questions.

1. What two baits can be combined to catch trout at San Pablo Lake?

   _____   _____

2. In Santa Cruz last week, how much did the biggest lingcod weigh?   _____

3. What fish in the 10-pound range were recently caught in the Pittsburg area near Isleton?   _____

4. At Parkway, what season is over until summer?   _____

5. What holiday mentioned in the Isleton listing suggests that this Fishing Guide was written in springtime?   _____

6. How much trout was recently planted in San Pablo Lake?   _____

RHYMING WORDS

Cross out two words in each group that do *not* rhyme with the **boldface** word.

1. **caught**   thought   drought   taut   talk

2. **coves**   doves   stoves   loaves   moves

3. **troll**   pole   coal   coil   owl

SYLLABLES

Divide each word in the box into syllables (separate sounds).

halibut
Sacramento
expected
combination
peninsula
Monterey

1. _____ / _____ / _____

_____ / _____ / _____

_____ / _____ / _____

2. _____ / _____ / _____ / _____

_____ / _____ / _____ / _____

_____ / _____ / _____ / _____

SYNONYMS

Write a letter to match each **boldface** word from the Fishing Guide with its *synonym* (word with the same meaning).

1. _____ **anglers**   a. trailing

2. _____ **spotty**   b. irregular

3. _____ **drifting**   c. allowed amounts

4. _____ **limits**   d. fishers

DRAWING CONCLUSIONS

Use information in the Fishing Guide to answer the questions.

1. What word in the Fishing Guide is a
    short way of saying "striped bass"?   _____

2. Are Broken Back Rebels and Mooselook
    likely to be lures or live bait?   _____

PUZZLER

Use the clues to complete the crossword puzzle.

ACROSS

3. period of time when
    something is permitted,
    or at its best

5. rising land at the edge
    of a body of water

6. to fish with a revolving
    lure trailing behind a
    moving boat

7. ridge of rock, coral,
    or sand just below
    the water's surface

8. food put on a hook
    to attract fish

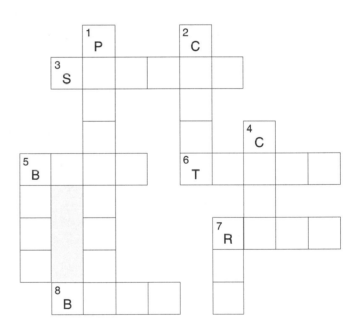

DOWN

1. land area projecting out
    into the water

2. seashore

4. small bay or inlet

5. small, open watercraft;
    vessel

7. fishing pole with a line,
    hook, and usually a reel

COMMUNITY CENTERS

Before reading. . .

Local community centers offer many low-cost opportunities for recreation and entertainment. Newspapers often publish a weekly listing like this one.

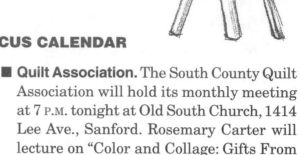

COMMUNITY FOCUS CALENDAR

THEATER/MUSIC

■ *Shall We Dance?* Sanford Symphony will perform "Shall We Dance?," a concert of dances drawn from classical music, 8 P.M. Saturday at Cox Center, 50 Greenleaf Blvd., Sanford. Tickets are $18–$41. Call 200-2000.

■ **Noon Concerts.** The Wiley Community Museum offers free concerts of classical and favorite selections at noon Fridays at Memorial Hall in the Wiley Town Center. Call 100-0001 or 100-1000.

■ *When El Cucui Walks.* Teatro Vision's production about romance and familial duty runs through Sunday at the Mexican Heritage Plaza Theatre, Wiley. Performances are 8 P.M. on Saturday, 2 and 7 P.M. on Sunday. Tickets are $8–$25. Call 100-2002

■ *The Music Man.* Homestead High School Drama Group will present this musical through June 3 at the Sanford Civic Theater. Performances are 8 P.M. on Saturday, 2:30 P.M. on Sunday. Tickets are $20. Call 200-0000.

CLUBS/GROUPS

■ **Spanish Book Club.** "Conversando Sobre Libros" book club meets at 6:30 P.M. Monday, as well as the last Monday of each month, at Biblioteca Latinoamericana Branch Library, 222 Grand Ave., Wiley. This month's book discussion will be "Casi Un Objeto" by José Saramago. Call 100-4321.

■ **Quilt Association.** The South County Quilt Association will hold its monthly meeting at 7 P.M. tonight at Old South Church, 1414 Lee Ave., Sanford. Rosemary Carter will lecture on "Color and Collage: Gifts From a Garden." Cost is $3. Call 200-0102.

■ **Scriptwriters Alliance.** The Westside chapter of this group for writers of novels, movies, and television meets from 9 to 11 A.M. the third Saturday of each month. Call 200-1111 for meeting locations.

YOUTH/FAMILY

■ **Kids Art Sunday.** The Flamenco Society will perform at the Wiley Museum of Art's "Kids' Art Sunday: Without Boundaries," 11 A.M. to 3 P.M. Sunday at 100 S. Market St., Wiley. The event also includes hands-on art workshops based on current exhibitions. Admission is free with museum admission, which is $7 adults, $4 seniors/students/youths 6–17. Call 100-1111.

■ **Let's Go to Disneyland!** The city of Marlow Parks and Recreation Department is planning a trip to Disneyland for middle and high school students on Aug. 21. Cost, which includes transportation, is $95 for Marlow residents, $118 for nonresidents. Call 300-1000 to register.

■ *Brave Little Tailor.* Sanford Civic Theater Group will perform an adaptation of this children's fairy tale, for grades K through 5, through June 2 at the Sanford Community Center. Performances for schools are at 9:30 and 11 A.M.

CLASSES AND LECTURES

■ **Museum Comedy Club.** The Wiley Community Museum will hold "Comedy Standup" practice from 7 to 8 P.M. Thursdays at the Wiley Town Center. Call 100-3003.

■ **Care for the Elderly.** Case Management for Elders will hold a class on "Death and Dying," 2 to 4 P.M. today at 8765 First St., Marlow. Cost is $5. Call 300-3333.

■ **ESL and Citizenship Classes.** Adult Education will hold a free six-week summer session in English as a Second Language (ESL) and Citizenship Preparation, beginning June 19 at Baker Middle School, 55 Taylor St., Sanford. Call 200-1000 by June 1 to register.

■ **Adult Ballet Classes.** The School of Modern Ballet is offering adult morning classes at the school, located at 40 N. Pine St., Wiley. Beginning Ballet is held from 9:30 to 11 A.M. Tuesdays, Intermediate Ballet from 9:30 to 11 A.M. Thursdays. Call 100-2121 for cost.

ART/EXHIBITS

■ **Train Presentations.** Antique working electric train sets are on display at the Wiley Community Museum from 2 to 4 P.M. Wednesdays until July 1. The exhibit includes activities, videos, and stories. Admission is free. Call 100-0001.

■ **Juried Art Show.** The Marlow Annual Open Juried Art Show will be on exhibit through Sunday at the Marlow Museum of Art and Natural History. Museum hours are 12 to 4 P.M. Wednesdays–Sundays. Call 300-3333.

■ **Student Exhibit.** Artworks created by students in Wiley Museum's ArtReach program, which brings visual arts instruction to public schools, hospitals, and senior centers, will be on display through Sunday at the Community Art Gallery, located behind Wiley Museum of Art. Gallery hours are from 12 to 4 P.M. Saturdays and Sundays.

MISCELLANEOUS

■ **Student Exchange.** The City of Marlow and the Yudo Sister City Organization will hold their Student Exchange Program July 24 through Aug. 14. Four Marlow students will stay in the homes of Japanese exchange students as Sister City student ambassadors. For information and applications, call Ed Ames at 300-2131.

FESTIVALS/EVENTS

■ **International Night.** The "All Shades of Colors" Club of Homestead High School will hold an International Night from 6:30 to 10 P.M. Saturday at the Sanford Community Center. The event includes Hawaiian, Asian, African, and Russian dance groups, hip-hop dance routines, food, live music, and a fashion show. Tickets are $5. Call 200-2030.

■ **Crab Fest.** Marlow High School's football team will hold a benefit Crab Fest from 5 to 10 P.M. Saturday at the Orchard City Banquet Hall, Community Center, 50500 Park Ave. The evening includes music, a sports memorabilia auction, and all-you-can-eat crab and clam chowder. Cost is $35. Call 300-4321.

*Want your event listed? Mail notices about general interest events **two weeks** in advance to Community Focus Calendar, Lincoln Park Drive, Sanford. Calendar items are published as space is available and not guaranteed. No permanent listings, commercial groups, or private businesses. Include the full name and telephone number for publication of someone who knows details.*

COMPREHENSION

Write **T** or **F** if the statement is *true* or *false*. Write **NI** if there is *no information* in the reading to help you make a judgment.

1. _____ The Marlow Parks and Recreation Department is planning a trip to Disneyland.

2. _____ Citizenship classes are being held at the Wiley Community Museum.

3. _____ Nothing is scheduled next month at the Mexican Heritage Plaza Theatre.

4. _____ Membership in the South County Quilt Association is for adults only.

5. _____ Free concerts will be held on Fridays at Memorial Hall in Wiley.

6. _____ There are no activities listed for people who don't speak English.

SENTENCE COMPLETION

Unscramble the **boldface** words from the reading to complete the sentences.

1. An **NICUTOA** _____ will be held at the Orchard City Banquet Hall.

2. All-you-can-eat crab and clam **WORDECH** _____ will be served.

3. Hip-hop **NECAD** _____ routines will be included in the performance.

4. Antique electric train sets will be on **LIDYAPS** _____.

5. An **TAPAIDNOTA** _____ of a children's fairy tale will be performed.

6. The drama group will present a **CUSLAMI** _____ called *The Music Man*.

SYLLABLES

Say the words from the reading out loud. Then divide each word into syllables (separate sounds).

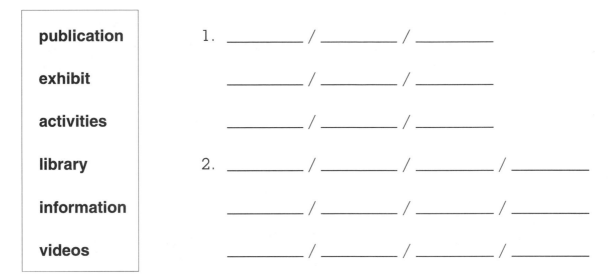

publication	1. _____ / _____ / _____
exhibit	_____ / _____ / _____
activities	_____ / _____ / _____
library	2. _____ / _____ / _____ / _____
information	_____ / _____ / _____ / _____
videos	_____ / _____ / _____ / _____

RHYMING WORDS

Cross out the word in each group that does *not* rhyme with the **boldface** word.

1. beginning **ballet** classes

   relay   mallet

   sleigh   buffet

2. events for **youth**

   truth   mouth

   booth   sleuth

3. the **group** will meet

   droop   soup

   grope   troupe

4. **high** school students

   dye   untie

   spry   height

DRAWING CONCLUSIONS

1. How much will it cost an 18-year-old to attend "Kids Art Sunday"? _____

2. Which group of students at Marlow High School will benefit from money made at the Crab Fest? _____

3. What is the last day you can see *The Music Man*? _____

4. Is Wiley's Community Art Gallery open during evening hours? _____

5. Residents of which city can buy the least expensive tickets for the trip to Disneyland? _____

6. School performances of *Brave Little Tailor* are being presented to which grades? _____

PUZZLER

Use the clues to solve the crossword puzzle.

ACROSS

3. building for displaying objects in art, science, history, etc.

5. an exhibit; something spread out to be seen

6. to move the body and feet in rhythm, often to music

7. something changed to a more suitable form

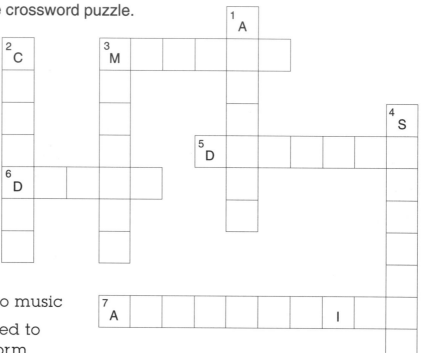

DOWN

1. sale at which each thing is sold to the highest bidder

2. thick soup made of fish with onions, potatoes, milk, etc.

3. play with songs and dances as well as spoken words

4. long piece of music for a full orchestra

VOCABULARY

Circle a letter to show the meaning of the **boldface** word or words.

1. **Hands-on** art workshops for children will be included in the event.

    a. finger painting and clay modeling

    b. touching famous artworks

    c. different kinds of active participation

2. Sports **memorabilia** will be auctioned.

   a. souvenirs of historic persons or events   b. informal, informative notes and letters   c. great moments that are still remembered

3. Antique working electric train sets will be **on display**.

   a. on loan   b. exhibited   c. demonstrated

4. International Night will include a fashion show and **live music**.

   a. a lively disk jockey   b. musicians on site   c. cheerful melodies

5. Romance and **familial duty** are the themes of the theater production.

   a. obligations to one's family   b. familiar characters   c. the duties of famous people

6. *Brave Little Tailor* will be presented by the Sanford **Civic** Theater Group.

   a. civilized, polite   b. governmentally approved   c. of the city of Sanford

SUFFIXES

Add the correct *suffix* from the box to each **boldface** word. Rewrite each word on the line. Hint: You will *not* use all the suffixes in the box.

-al	-ial	-ly	-ual	-ence	-ion	-sion	-ing	-ed

1. The class called "Death and **(Die)** _____" will be held today.

2. The concert will feature dances drawn from **(classic)** _____ music.

3. The Quilt **(Associate)** _____ will hold its monthly meeting at 7 P.M.

4. **(Commerce)** _____ groups may not advertise events in the Community Focus Calendar.

5. Wiley Museum's Art Reach program brings **(vision)** _____ arts instruction to schools.

6. José Saramago will lead this month's book **(discuss)** _____.

CYCLING

Before reading . . .

Riding a bicycle is a great way to get out and enjoy yourself. In addition, cycling provides convenient, low-cost transportation and excellent exercise.

CYCLING DOs AND DON'Ts

- DO pedal with the ball of your foot, not the heel or the arch.

- DO add aluminum bar end if you use flat handle bars. (Bar ends reduce arm fatigue.)

- DO adjust your bike to fit you! Be sure your seat is high enough. When a leg is fully extended, your heel should rest on the bottom pedal.

- DO mount the bike by stepping up on the top pedal; get off by stepping from the bottom pedal as you come to a stop.

- DON'T torture yourself by staying in one gear. Learn to use all your gears, and shift often.

- DON'T use too high a gear during your first rides; downshifting prevents strain and fatigue.

WHAT KIND OF BICYCLE IS RIGHT FOR YOU?

Road Bikes

A road bike has a lightweight frame and hard, narrow, high-pressure tires. The "drop" handlebars put the rider in a forward-leaning position. Road bikes are not recommended for travel on rough roads.

Road bike variants:

- *Racing bikes* have ultralight frames and racing equipment.

- *Touring bikes* are designed for travelers or commuters who carry heavy packs.

- *Ten-speed bikes*, especially inexpensive ones with heavy frames and inadequate gears, can be very uncomfortable to ride.

Mountain Bikes

Mountain bikes may be either medium or light in weight. They all have wide, soft tires. Some have shock absorbers. The rider on a mountain bike leans forward slightly.

If a mountain bike is ridden on streets instead of trails, its knobby tires should be replaced with smooth-rolling "slicks."

Hybrid Bikes

A hybrid bike may be medium or light in weight. Its tires are fatter than a road bike's, but narrower than a mountain bike's. The rider sits upright.

What Size Bike Is Right for You?

Stand over the bike with your feet together.

If your bike is a road bike, the top tube should come up to your crotch. If your bike is a hybrid or mountain bike, the top tube should be about two inches below your crotch.

YEAR 2001 BIKES, HERE NOW!

CLOSEOUT

THE BIKE LANE SPRING SPECIALS UP TO 50% OFF

Bicycle Specials Limited in Frame, Size and Colors.

'00 Specialized Hardrock Comp
- 24-Speed Mtn. Bike
- Shimano
- Chrome Molly
$349 Value   SAVE $100   **$249**

▶▶ Specialized ▶▶ GT
▶▶ Schwinn ▶▶ Diamondback

Diamondback Response Mtn. Bike
- Alum. Frame
- Shimano Gear System
- $319 Value
SAVE $70   **$249**

Schwinn ProStock 3
- BMX Racing
- Alum. Frame
- $299 Value
SAVE $100   **$199**

Specialized Hardrock Comp A1
- 24-Speed Mtn. Bike
- Rock Shox
- Shimano Decore
- $500 Value
SAVE $51   **$449**

Specialized Allez Sport
- 27-Speed Road Bike
- Shimano Ultegra
- $1399 Value
SAVE $400   **$999**

Specialized FSR Comp
- Dual Suspension Rock Shox
- Shimano XT Derailers
- $1349 Value
SAVE $350   **$999**

Specialized Crossroads
- 21-Speed Hybrid
- Shimano Gears
- $299 Value
SAVE $50   **$249**

1505 MAIN STREET HOMETOWN, KANSAS

OPEN DAILY 10-7.
SAT. 9-6. SUN. 12-5

Guaranteed Lowest Prices
If you find a lower advertised price, just bring in the ad and we will beat it. Must be currently in other dealer's stock.

THE BIKE LANE
SINCE 1972
BICYCLES SALES + ACCESSORIES
MasterCard   VISA

CYCLING FOR FITNESS

A good fitness goal is to ride at 12 miles an hour or more (on level ground) for at least 30 minutes, four or five days a week. This program will greatly increase your heart and lung capacity. It will also develop leg muscle strength as well as flexibility in the hips, knees, and ankles.

THE FIRST BIKE

The "grandfather" of the modern bicycle was called a *velocipede*. It became popular in France about 1855. The frame and wheels were made of wood. The tires were iron. The front wheel was slightly higher than the back wheel. In England, the velocipede became known as the "boneshaker" because of the effect it had on a rider pedaling over a rough road.

READING AN AD

Find information in the ad to answer the questions.

1. What bicycle store is
   offering a special sale? _____

2. What's the *least* expensive
   bicycle described in the ad? _____

3. What words do the abbreviations
   Alum. and *Mtn.* stand for? _____

4. Which bike is advertised at the *biggest* savings off the regular
   price? How much would you save?

   _____

5. Which mountain bike
   has 24 speeds? _____

6. Which bike advertised
   is a hybrid? _____

7. Which bike advertised
   is a racing bike? _____

8. Which bike in the advertisement offers the *least* savings?
   How much would you save?

   _____

MULTIPLE-MEANING WORDS

Many words have entirely different meanings when they're used in a different
context. Circle a letter to show the meaning of the **boldface** word as it is used
in the sentence.

1. A rider should **mount** the bike by stepping up on the top pedal.

   a. a mountain or hill   b. climb up on   c. paste in a scrapbook

2. Downshifting prevents **strain** and fatigue.

   a. weakening by too much force   b. passing through a filter   c. an inherited quality

3. A cycle shop called The Bike Lane will **beat** any price.

   a. to hit repeatedly   b. mark time in music   c. offer a better deal

4. The top **tube** should be two inches below your crotch.

   a. container for glue, toothpaste, etc.   b. hollow metal bar on a bike frame   c. air-filled rubber ring in a tire

PUZZLER

Use the clues to help you solve the crossword puzzle. Answers are words that complete the sentences.

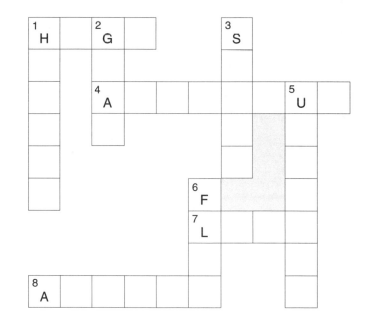

ACROSS

1. Don't use too _____ a gear on your first rides.

4. Add _____ bar ends to flat handlebars.

7. Biking builds heart and _____ capacity.

8. Be sure to _____ your bike seat to the right height.

DOWN

1. A _____ bike has fatter tires than a road bike.

2. Don't torture yourself by staying in one _____.

3. Learn to use all your gears and _____ often.

5. The cyclist sits _____ on a hybrid bike.

6. Bar ends should be attached to _____ handlebars.

SYLLABLES

Divide each word in the box into syllables (the separate sounds in a word).

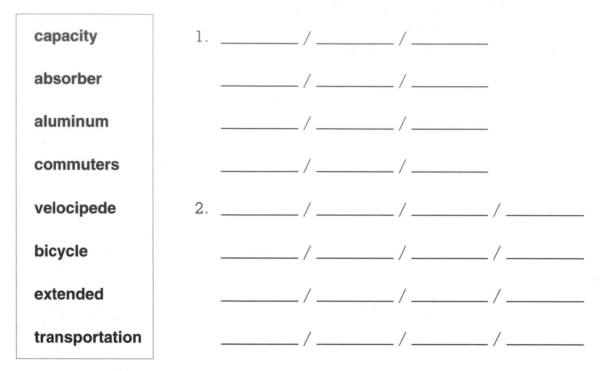

capacity	1. _____ / _____ / _____
absorber	_____ / _____ / _____
aluminum	_____ / _____ / _____
commuters	_____ / _____ / _____
velocipede	2. _____ / _____ / _____ / _____
bicycle	_____ / _____ / _____ / _____
extended	_____ / _____ / _____ / _____
transportation	_____ / _____ / _____ / _____

VOCABULARY

Notice the **boldface** word or words in each phrase from the reading. Then circle a letter to show what it means.

1. When a leg is **fully extended**

    a. heavily muscled   b. stretched out   c. completely grown

2. with the **ball** of your foot

    a. the rounded part   b. a pitch that   c. clenched toes
        just below the toes   is not a strike   making a fist

3. road bike **variants**

    a. variety   b. including racing bikes   c. different kinds
        of colors   and mountain bikes   of road bikes

4. replace its **knobby** tires

    a. like a handle   b. rough and   c. smooth,
        on a drawer   bumpy   rounded

28

WORD COMPLETION

Add vowels (*a, e, i, o, u*) to complete the words.

1. T ___ ___ R ___ N G bikes are designed for travelers who carry heavy packs.

2. Don't use too high a G ___ ___ R during your first rides.

3. The velocipede was called a "B ___ N ___ S H ___ K ___ R" because of its rough ride.

4. Biking develops F L ___ X ___ B ___ L ___ T Y in the hips, knees, and ankles.

5. R ___ ___ D bikes are not recommended for travel on rough roads.

6. ___ N ___ X P ___ N S ___ V ___ 10-speed bikes can be very uncomfortable to ride.

COMPOUND WORDS

Use a word from the box to complete the compound word in each sentence.
Hint: You will *not* use all the words in the box.

down	**up**	**heavy**	**light**	**in**
handle	**out**	**grade**	**shift**	

1. A road bike's "drop" _____**bars** put the rider in a forward-leaning position.

2. When you **down**_____, you prevent strain and fatigue.

3. A **close**_____ sale is currently being held at The Bike Lane.

4. A road bike has narrow, high-pressure tires and a _____**weight** frame.

5. On a hybrid bike, the rider sits in an _____**right** position.

Unit 1
REVIEW

WORD COMPLETION

Add vowels (*a, e, i, o, u*) to complete the words.

1. ESL and C __ T __ Z __ N S H __ P classes are often held at neighborhood community centers.

2. Stamps that honor important people and events are called C __ MM __ M __ R __ T __ V __ S.

3. __ N G L __ R S are interested to learn where their favorite fish are biting.

4. Regular biking develops F L __ X __ B __ L __ T Y in the hips, knees, and ankles.

SPECIALIZED VOCABULARY

Match the example terms in the box with the headings below. Write the examples on the lines.

shock absorbers	watermarks	exhibition	mint
trollers	perforations	production	tube
memorabilia	variants	drifting	limits

1.   **FISHING GUIDE**

_____

_____

_____

3.   **CYCLING**

_____

_____

_____

2.   **COMMUNITY CENTERS**

_____

_____

_____

4.   **COLLECTING STAMPS**

_____

_____

_____

GOOD COOKING

LESSON 1: The Language of Cooking

LESSON 2: Food Safety

LESSON 3: Microwave Cooking

LESSON 4: Cooking Outdoors

When you complete this unit, you will be able to answer questions like these:

■ *What is the first rule of food safety?*

■ *What's the difference between chopping and dicing?*

■ *After lighting charcoal briquets, how long should you wait before cooking?*

■ *How can you make sure that foods cook evenly in a microwave oven?*

PRETEST

Write **T** or **F** to show whether you think each statement is *true* or *false*.

1. _____ It is never safe to immediately place hot food in the refrigerator.

2. _____ Egg whites form stiff peaks if they stand up straight when the beaters are lifted from the bowl.

3. _____ It takes about 45 minutes to cook raw chicken in a microwave oven.

4. _____ Wind and air temperature affect the length of time it takes to grill food outdoors.

5. _____ In a microwave, covering food with plastic wrap speeds heating.

6. _____ You will overfill a standard size grill if you use more than 20 briquets.

Pretest answers: 1. F 2. T 3. F 4. T 5. T 6. F

THE LANGUAGE OF COOKING

Before reading . . .

Almost every art and skill has its own vocabulary. In this lesson you will study the special terms used in recipes.

Bake: Cook in oven.

Baste: To keep food moist, spoon a liquid over food during cooking.

Beat: Mix ingredients vigorously until smooth. Use a spoon, hand beater, or electric mixer.

Blanch: Plunge food briefly into boiling water. Blanching is done in order to preserve color, texture, and nutritional value—or to remove skins from fruits or nuts.

Boil: Heat until bubbles rise continuously and break on the surface; for *rolling boil,* heat until the bubbles form rapidly.

Chop: Cut into irregular pieces. Use a sharp knife, food chopper, or food processor.

Coat: Cover food evenly with crumbs or a sauce.

Cool: Allow hot food to come to room temperature.

Crisp-Tender: Food cooked until it is tender but still retains some of the crisp texture of the raw food.

Crush: Grind into fine particles. Crush clove of garlic, for example, using chef's knife or garlic press.

Cube: Cut into three-dimensional squares ½ inch (or larger) with knife.

Cut In: Use a rolling motion with a pastry blender to distribute fat in dry ingredients. Alternatively, cutting with two knives until particles are desired size.

Dash: Less than ⅛ teaspoon of an ingredient.

Dice: Cut into cubes smaller than ½ inch square.

Finely Chopped: Cut into very tiny pieces.

Flake: Separate into pieces with fork, as in flaking fish.

Fold: Combine ingredients lightly, using two motions. First, cut vertically through mixture with rubber spatula. Next, slide spatula across bottom of bowl and up the side, turning the mixture over. Continue down-across-up-over motion while rotating bowl ¼ turn with each series of strokes.

Garnish: Before serving, decorate the food with additional foods that have distinctive color or texture, such as parsley, fresh berries, or carrot curls.

Glaze: Brush or drizzle a mixture on a food to give it a glossy appearance, hard finish, or decoration.

Grate: Cut into tiny particles using the small holes of a grater or a food processor.

Marinate: Let food stand in a savory (usually acidic) liquid for several hours to add flavor or to tenderize. *Marinade* is the savory liquid in which the food is marinated.

Mix: Combine ingredients in any way that distributes them evenly.

Pan-Fry: Beginning with a cold skillet, fry food in little or no fat.

Pare: Cut off outer covering with knife or vegetable parer (examples: apples or pears).

Peel: Use fingers to strip off outer covering (examples: bananas or oranges).

Refrigerate: Place food in refrigerator to chill or store.

Roast: Cook uncovered meat in oven on rack in shallow pan without adding liquid.

Sauté: Cook foods in hot oil or melted butter or margarine over medium-high heat with frequent tossing and turning motion.

Scald: Heat liquid to just below the boiling point, or until tiny bubbles form at the edges.

Score: Cut surface of food about ¼ inch deep with knife to facilitate cooking, flavoring, or tenderizing.

Shred: Cut into long, thin pieces. Use a knife or the large holes of a grater or a food processor.

Simmer: Continue to heat to just below boiling. Bubbles will rise slowly and break just below the surface. Usually done after reducing heat from boiling point.

Slice: Cut into uniform flat pieces.

Soft Peaks: Egg whites beaten until peaks curl when beaters are lifted from bowl, but eggs are still moist and glossy.

Soften: Let food such as margarine, butter, or cream cheese stand at room temperature, or microwave at medium-low (30 percent heat) until soft.

Stiff Peaks: Egg whites beaten until peaks stand up straight when beaters are lifted from bowl, but eggs are still moist and glossy.

Stir: Mix ingredients with circular or figure-eight motion until the mix is uniform in consistency.

Stir-Fry: A Chinese method of cooking uniform pieces of food. Place food in small amount of oil over high heat, stirring constantly.

Tear: Use fingers to break into pieces.

Toss: Tumble ingredients lightly with a lifting motion.

COMPREHENSION

Write **T** or **F** if the statement is *true* or *false*. Write **NI** if there is *no information* in the reading to help you make a judgment.

1. _____ *Grated* food is cut into smaller pieces than *diced* food.

2. _____ *Marinating* food before cooking is a method invented by the Chinese.

3. _____ A *dash* of pepper is about half a teaspoon.

4. _____ You must *blanch* a tomato if you want the skin to peel off easily.

5. _____ A *rubber spatula* is the right tool to help you combine ingredients lightly.

SUFFIXES

Rewrite the **boldface** word in each sentence, adding one of the suffixes in the box. Hint: You will *not* use all the suffixes.

-ize	-ly	-ous	-or	-al	-ion	-ist	-er

1. You can **(tender)** _____ and add flavor to food by marinating it.

2. When you stir-fry food, you must stir it **(constant)** _____.

3. You can use a food **(process)** _____ to shred food.

4. Diced cubes are **(small)** _____ than ½ inch square.

5. Berries are sometimes used as **(decorate)** _____ on a dessert plate.

6. Blanching food can help to maintain its **(nutrition)** _____ value.

7. When liquid is boiling, the rise of bubbles will be **(continue)** _____.

SYLLABLES

Say the words from the reading out loud. Then divide each word into *syllables* (separate sounds).

processor	texture	distinctive	simmer	particles	solid

1. _____ / _____

_____ / _____

_____ / _____

2. _____ / _____ / _____

_____ / _____ / _____

_____ / _____ / _____

PUZZLER

Use the clues to help you solve the crossword puzzle. Answers are words that complete the sentences.

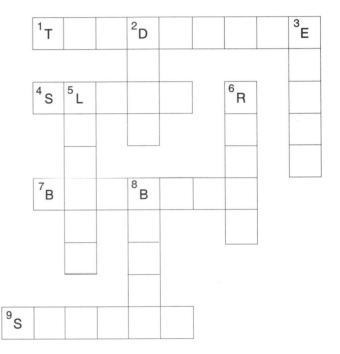

ACROSS

1. Marinade can be used to ___ food.

4. When you ___ food, you cut it into flat pieces.

7. When you see ___, you know that water is boiling.

9. To ___ food is to continue to heat it just below the boiling point.

DOWN

2. When you ___ a vegetable, you cut it into very small cubes.

3. Tiny bubbles form at the ___ of scalded liquid.

5. A marinade is not a solid, but a ___.

6. To ___ a turkey, cook it uncovered in a shallow pan.

8. You ___ food to keep it moist while cooking.

PLURALS

Write the *plural* (names more than one) form of each word from the reading.

1. bubble _____

2. berry _____

3. knife _____

4. dish _____

VOCABULARY

Circle a letter to show the meaning of each **boldface** word.

1. Drizzling glaze on a cake gives it a **glossy** appearance.

   a. crisp and golden
   b. smooth and shiny
   c. fragrant and delicious

2. Cut the surface of meat about one inch deep to **facilitate** cooking.

   a. help; make easier
   b. double the amount
   c. extend; lengthen

3. Use a knife to cut cubes into **three-dimensional** squares.

   a. backward, forward, and sideways
   b. triangular; three-sided
   c. having depth as well as height and width

4. Food may be blanched to **preserve** color.

   a. keep from rotting or spoiling
   b. maintain or protect
   c. pickle with salt or vinegar

5. To marinate food is to let it stand in a **savory** liquid for several hours before cooking it.

   a. pleasing to taste or smell
   b. very salty or sour
   c. no warmer than room temperature

6. Parsley and carrot curls are often used to **garnish** food.

   a. season or add flavor to
   b. decorate or enhance
   c. marinate or soak

WORD COMPLETION

Add vowels (*a, e, i, o, u*) to complete the words.

1. To blend __ NGR __ D __ __ NTS, stir until the mixture is smooth.

2. By grating food, you cut it into tiny P __ RT __ CL __ S.

3. Properly beaten egg whites are M __ __ ST and glossy.

4. Before stir-frying, cut food into __ N __ F __ RM pieces.

5. To soften M __ RG __ R __ N __, let it stand at room temperature.

6. To C __ __ T food means to cover it with crumbs or a sauce.

SYNONYMS

Draw a line to match each **boldface** word from the reading with its *synonym* (word that means the same or nearly the same).

1. **consistency**   a. mix

2. **skillet**   b. frying pan

3. **uniform**   c. thickness

4. **combine**   d. identical

CATEGORIES

Unscramble the *verbs* (action words). Then list each word under the correct heading.

P O C H _____	1. **HEATING METHODS**
D A L C S _____	_____
S O T S _____	_____
P E A R _____	_____
D O L F _____	_____
S T O A R _____	2. **CUTTING METHODS**
D R E S H _____	_____
U T S É A _____	_____
I X M _____	_____
C I D E _____	_____
K A B E _____	3. **STIRRING METHODS**
C I L E S _____	_____
	_____
	_____

FOOD SAFETY

Before reading . . .

Bacteria can spoil food and even cause deadly food poisoning. That's why the first rule of food safety is to keep hot foods *hot* and cold foods *cold*. The second rule is to keep everything in the kitchen *clean*—because most bacteria get into food through careless handling.

Keeping Food Hot or Cold

HOT FOODS CHECKLIST

- Use a meat thermometer to make sure that meat and poultry are cooked thoroughly.

- Don't interrupt cooking. Cook meat and poultry to final "doneness" at one time.

- Bring gravy to a rolling boil before serving.

- Never leave food out longer than two hours.

The most perishable foods are those containing eggs, milk (such as creamed foods and cream pies), seafood, meat, and poultry. When you shop, pick up your meat and poultry selections last. Take them straight home and refrigerate.

Bacteria thrive in lukewarm food. Don't allow hot or cold foods to remain at room temperature for more than two hours, including preparation time. A standard rule, recommended by the U.S. Department of Agriculture, is to keep hot foods above 140°F and cold foods below 40°F.

Once food has been cooked, keep it hot until serving, or refrigerate as soon as possible. If it will not raise the refrigerator temperature above 45°, hot food can be placed immediately in the refrigerator.

Keeping the Kitchen Clean

■ Germs are a natural part of the environment. Keep countertops, appliances, utensils, and dishes sanitary. Do this by cleaning with water and soap or other cleansers.

■ Wash hands thoroughly with soap and water. Wear protective plastic gloves. If you have any kind of cut or infection on your hands, don't handle food.

■ Be careful not to transfer germs from raw meat to cooked meat. Example: Do not carry raw hamburgers to the grill on a platter, and then serve cooked meat on the same, unwashed platter.

■ Do not use wooden cutting boards for raw meat or poultry. A hard plastic cutting board is less porous and safer for meats. It can also be easily cleaned or washed in a dishwasher. Wash boards after each use. Use a mixture of two teaspoons chlorine bleach and one teaspoon vinegar to one gallon of water.

■ Wash the meat keeper and crisper drawer of your refrigerator often. Keep containers for storing refrigerated food very clean.

■ Use disposable paper towels when working with or cleaning up after raw foods.

How Long Does Food Stay Fresh?

- *Raw poultry, fish, and meat:* two to three days in the refrigerator, three to six months in the freezer

- *Raw ground meat or poultry:* one to two days in the refrigerator, three months in the freezer

- *Cooked whole roasts or whole poultry:* two to three days in the refrigerator, nine months in the freezer

- *Cooked poultry pieces:* one to two days in the refrigerator, one month in the freezer

- *Bread:* three months in the freezer

- *Ice cream:* one to two months

- *Soups and stews:* two to three days in the refrigerator, one to three months in the freezer

- *Casseroles:* two to three days in the refrigerator, one to three months in the freezer

- *Cookies:* six to eight months in the freezer

- *Baking powder:* six months tightly sealed at room temperature

- *Baking soda:* 18 months fairly well-covered at room temperature

- *Bouillon cubes:* 1 year at room temperature

- *Peanut butter:* one year, unopened, at room temperature; three to four months after opening, stored in the refrigerator

- *Salt:* indefinitely; up to one year for seasoned salt; stored tightly capped at room temperature

- *Soy sauce:* up to one year, unopened, at room temperature; one year after opening if refrigerated

- *Spices and dried herbs:* up to one year if whole and stored tightly capped on a cool shelf; six months if ground; store red spices such as paprika, ground red pepper, and chili powder in the refrigerator or freezer, along with poppy seeds or sesame seeds, which can become rancid.

- *Vinegar:* indefinitely if unopened; six months once opened at room temperature

- *Extracts:* three to four months tightly sealed at room temperature

- *Honey:* indefinitely if tightly sealed; if it has crystallized, place opened jar in bowl of hot water and stir until crystals dissolve

---

STORAGE TIPS

- Writes dates on leftovers or things going into the freezer.

- Pay attention to "sell by" dates and expiration dates.

- Don't use anything that you're unsure of. Leftovers should be refrigerated immediately.

- Store restaurant leftovers in resealable plastic bags rather than their foam containers.

- Group leftovers together so you can see what you have.

- Keep things that you use most often at the front of shelves.

COMPREHENSION

Write **T** or **F** if the statement is *true* or *false.* Write **NI** if there is *no information* in the reading to help you make a judgment.

1. _____ Any food in an unopened package will stay fresh for a year.

2. _____ Plastic cutting boards are safer than wooden cutting boards.

3. _____ Cold foods will stay cold at a temperature of 40°F.

4. _____ Uncooked hamburger will stay fresh in the refrigerator for four or five days.

5. _____ Leftover creamed chicken should be thrown away immediately.

6. _____ If kept frozen, a cake will stay fresh for six months.

SUFFIXES

Rewrite the **boldface** words by adding a suffix from the box. Hint: You will *not* use all the suffixes in the box.

-ive	-able	-ion	-ed	-ly	-ant	-ation

1. Don't handle food if you have an **(infect)** _____ on your hands.

2. It's a good idea to wear **(protect)** _____ plastic gloves when you handle food.

3. Use **(dispose)** _____ paper towels when working with raw foods.

4. If tightly sealed, honey may be stored **(indefinite)** _____.

5. Spices should be stored tightly **(cap)** _____ on a cool shelf.

6. Pay close attention to **(expire)** _____ dates stamped on food packages.

PUZZLER

Use the clues to help you solve the crossword puzzle. Answers are words from the reading.

ACROSS

4. one-celled living things that can cause disease

5. coverings for the hands

6. to grow in a strong, healthy way

7. measurement of heat level

DOWN

1. device for measuring temperature

2. to heat liquid until it bubbles up and becomes steam or vapor

3. likely to spoil or decay

4. chemical such as peroxide or chlorine used to whiten or sanitize

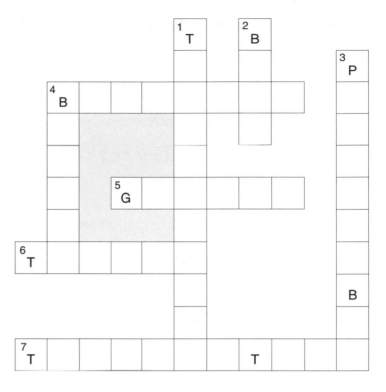

DRAWING CONCLUSIONS

Answer in complete sentences.

1. Why do you think restaurant leftovers should be stored in resealable plastic bags rather than their foam containers?

   _____

2. Why should gravy come to a rolling boil before being served?

   _____

3. What is a "sell by" date? Where would you see such a date?

   _____

   _____

SENTENCE COMPLETION

Unscramble the **boldface** words from the reading to complete the sentences.

1. Wash cutting boards with a mixture of water, bleach, and
   EVGRAIN _____.

2. Before serving, bring **VYRAG** _____ to a rolling boil.

3. When you shop, pick up your meat and **TROYLUP**
   _____ selections last.

4. Most bacteria get into food because of careless **GLINNAHD**
   _____.

5. Wash the meat **REPEEK** _____ drawer of your
   refrigerator often.

6. Casseroles can be kept in the **REEFREZ** _____
   for as long as four weeks.

COMPOUND WORDS

Write a compound word to correctly complete each sentence. Take the first part of the compound from Box A and the second part from Box B. Hint: You will *not* use all the words.

BOX A		
counter	sea	dish
left	right	luke

BOX B		
overs	towel	washer
food	warm	tops

1. Bacteria thrive in _____ food.

2. _____ must be refrigerated immediately.

3. Clean your _____ often to keep them germ-free.

4. A hard plastic cutting board can be cleaned in a
   _____.

5. Refrigerate _____ immediately after eating.

SYLLABLES

Say the words from the reading out loud. Then divide each word into syllables (separate sounds).

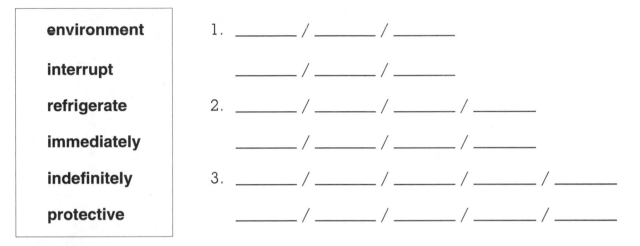

environment	1. _____ / _____ / _____
interrupt	_____ / _____ / _____
refrigerate	2. _____ / _____ / _____ / _____
immediately	_____ / _____ / _____ / _____
indefinitely	3. _____ / _____ / _____ / _____ / _____
protective	_____ / _____ / _____ / _____ / _____

ANTONYMS

Notice the **boldface** word in each sentence. Then circle that word's *antonym* (word that means the opposite) in the group of words below.

1. Sesame seeds can become **rancid** if they're not stored in the freezer.

   withered   hot   fresh   fragrant

2. Bacteria **thrive** in lukewarm food.

   die   multiply   flourish   mutate

3. Keep all appliances and utensils **sanitary**.

   white   scalded   dirty   safe

4. Wooden cutting boards are more **porous** than plastic ones.

   liquid   hard   sturdy   useful

5. Vanilla extract should be **sealed** at room temperature.

   labeled   approved   maintained   opened

6. Put a jar of honey in hot water and stir until the crystals **dissolve**.

   condense   disappear   liquify   crystallize

MICROWAVE COOKING

Before reading . . .

Microwave cooking has become very popular. Why? Because it is so quick and easy. The information in this lesson will help you to use this handy cooking appliance safely and effectively.

Basic Principles of Microwave Cooking

Temperature of Food: The colder the food, the longer the cooking time.

Volume of Food: As the amount of the food increases, so must the cooking time.

Size of Pieces of Food: Small pieces of food cook faster than large pieces. Keep pieces uniform in size to prevent uneven cooking.

Shape of Food: Round or doughnut-shaped foods— or foods in round or ring-shaped containers—cook most evenly. Irregular-shaped foods need more attention during cooking.

Density of Food: Porous foods (breads, cakes) cook quickly; dense foods (roasts, potatoes) need longer cooking.

Microwave Cooking Techniques

The following techniques help to ensure even cooking:

- Cover food tightly with a lid or plastic wrap to speed heating. Leave a corner or two-inch edge of plastic turned back.

- Cover food loosely with waxed paper or microwavable paper towel to prevent splatters.

- Stir by moving hot edges to the center.

- Rotate dish ½ or ¼ turn when cooking foods that cannot be stirred.

- Arrange foods in a circle for most even cooking.

- For more even cooking, turn foods over partway through cooking time.

- Microwave for the minimum time recommended in the recipe. Check for doneness before adding additional time.

- Elevate on an inverted dish to cook bottom center of very moist food.

- Cover uncooked food with a crumb or cracker coating, or brush on a sauce or glaze. This will add color and crispness.

Microwaving Chicken

Arrange chicken parts, skin sides up, in microwavable dish. Put thickest parts near the outside edge. Make sure the dish is large enough to hold all the pieces without overlapping. Cover and microwave until juices run clear. Cook the cut-up broiler-fryer (3 to $3\frac{1}{2}$ lbs.) on high for 15 to 20 minutes. Rotate dish one-half turn after 10 minutes.

Microwaving Fish

Use a shallow microwavable dish large enough to hold pieces in a single layer. Place the thickest parts close to the outside edges. Cover tightly and microwave on high until fish flakes easily with a fork. Cook one pound of fish fillets ($\frac{1}{2}$ to $\frac{3}{4}$ inch thick) from five to seven minutes. Rotate dish one-half turn after three minutes.

MICROWAVE SAFETY

- Avoid steam burns by opening hot containers away from the face and hands. To release steam, slowly lift the farthest edge of the cover. Open popcorn and other cooking bags away from the face.

- Use potholders to prevent burns from containers or utensils in contact with hot food. Heat from the food can transfer to the container and make it dangerously hot.

- Follow the instructions provided by the microwave oven manufacturer.

- Don't use metal containers that aren't specifically designed for microwave cooking.

COMPREHENSION

Write **T** or **F** if the statement is *true* or *false*. Write **NI** if there is *no information* in the reading to help you make a judgment.

1. _____ In microwave cooking, the power setting must increase as the amount of food increases.

2. _____ For more even cooking, turn foods over partway through the total cooking time.

45

3. _____ Both chicken and fish should be microwaved on the *high* power setting.

4. _____ The *low* power setting on a microwave should only be used for defrosting frozen foods.

5. _____ To heat thoroughly, the thickest pieces of food should be placed in the middle of the dish.

6. _____ Before microwaving, always add a little water to chicken or fish.

PUZZLER

Use the clues to help you solve the crossword puzzle. Answers are words that complete the sentences.

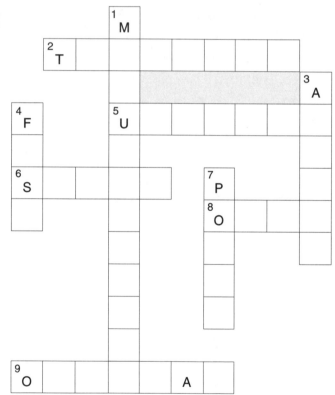

ACROSS

2. Heat from food can ___ to the container.

5. ___ pieces of food will cook evenly.

6. Open hot containers away from the face to avoid ___ burns.

8. A microwave ___ cooks food faster than a conventional oven.

9. Food pieces arranged in a single layer do not ___.

DOWN

1. Follow the directions given by the microwave ___.

3. As the ___ of food increases, so must the cooking time.

4. ___ is considered done when it flakes easily.

7. Cook one ___ of fish fillets five to seven minutes.

SYLLABLES

Say the words from the reading aloud. Then break each word into *syllables* (separate sounds) on the lines below.

| instructions | metal | containers | contact | potholders | plastic |

1. _____ / _____

_____ / _____

_____ / _____

2. _____ / _____ / _____

_____ / _____ / _____

_____ / _____ / _____

SPELLING

Circle the *misspelled* word in each sentence. Then write the words correctly on the lines.

1. Certain tekneeks ensure even cooking in a microwave oven.

_____

2. Before cooking, cover the food with a microwaveable paper towel.

_____

3. Cook foods for the minimum time reccomended in the recipe.

_____

4. Fish fillays are usually ½ to ¾ inch thick.

_____

5. Small peaces of food cook faster than large ones.

_____

WORD COMPLETION

Use vowels (*a, e, i, o, u*) to complete the words.

1. The microwave oven is a popular cooking __ P P L __ __ N C __.

2. Cooking time must increase as the V __ L __ M __ of food increases.

3. Brushing on a sauce adds an attractive C __ L __ R to food.

4. To prevent splatters, cover food L __ __ S __ LY with waxed paper.

5. Open P__ PC __ RN and other cooking bags away from the face.

6. An average BR __ __ L __ R-fryer chicken weighs about three pounds.

7. R __ __ ND containers cook food most evenly.

8. R __ T __ T __ the dish halfway through the total cooking time.

SYNONYMS AND ANTONYMS

Unscramble the words from the reading. Then complete each sentence with the correct word.

NEDLB _____	SNECHQUIET _____
EPDE _____	UMIXAMM _____
SOUPRO _____	RAILCRUC _____

1. A **shallow** dish is the opposite of a _____ dish.

2. The words **mix** and _____ are *synonyms*.

3. The words **dense** and _____ are *antonyms*.

4. A **round** dish could also be called _____.

5. Cooking **methods** or **procedures** could also be called

   _____.

6. The words **minimum** and _____ are opposites.

FORMS OF A WORD

Notice that the **boldface** word in each sentence is in the wrong *form*. Write the correct form of the word on the line after each sentence.

1. For more even cooking, **turning** foods over
   partway through the cooking time.   _____

2. Dense foods need to be cooked **longest**
   than porous foods do.   _____

48

3. To **allowance** steam to escape, turn back a corner of the plastic wrap.

_____

4. When **cooked** chicken, rotate the dish one-half turn after 10 minutes.

_____

5. Follow the **instructor** provided by the microwave manufacturer.

_____

6. Use potholders to **prevention** burns from contact with hot foods.

_____

RHYMING

Circle the word that does _not_ rhyme with each **boldface** word from the reading.

1. **stir**   stare   purr   blur   her

2. **food**   dude   blood   stewed   glued

3. **size**   sighs   tries   eyes   seize

4. **enough**   stuff   tough   although   gruff

SENTENCE COMPLETION

Write a letter to match the beginning of each sentence on the left with its correct ending on the right.

1. _____ Microwave fish until

2. _____ Very cold food

3. _____ To speed heating,

4. _____ For most even cooking,

5. _____ Don't use metal containers

a. arrange foods in a circle.

b. takes longer to cook than warm food.

c. it flakes easily with a fork.

d. that aren't specifically designed for the microwave.

e. cover food with plastic wrap.

COOKING OUTDOORS

Before reading . . .

Cooking outdoors was once a special summertime treat. Today, people enjoy grilling foods all year around. This lesson provides some useful tips to help you use an outdoor grill skillfully and safely.

USING CHARCOAL BRIQUETTES

1. Do not overfill your grill. Use about 40 briquettes in a standard-size grill.

2. Stack briquettes and light with a match in several places. Never use lighter fluid. Do not cover flaming briquettes with the grill lid.

3. Wait for flames to die out. When briquettes are completely ashed over, spread evenly in grill and begin cooking.

Great Grilling!

• The type of grill, outdoor temperature, and wind can affect cooking times. For best results, check the food and fire often.

• Whether a gas, electric, or charcoal grill is used, it's important to keep the heat as even as possible throughout the grilling period.

• If you're not getting a "sizzle," the fire may be too cool. Regulate the heat by spreading the coals or raking them together. You can also open or close the vents or adjust the control on a gas or electric grill. Raising, lowering, or covering the cooking grill is another way to help control the heat.

• Use wood chips to add a smoky flavor to grilled foods. Soak hickory, mesquite, green hardwood, or fruitwood chips in water for 30 minutes. Then drain and toss on the hot coals.

• For a different flavor and aroma, sprinkle the hot coals with soaked and drained dried herbs, fresh herbs, or garlic cloves.

• Long-handled barbecue tools allow for safe distance between you and intense heat. Use a brush for adding sauces or marinades before or during grilling. But once the food is cooked, the brush should not be used to add additional sauce. This prevents transferring any bacteria from the uncooked food to the cooked food. Wash the brush in hot, soapy water and dry thoroughly.

- Be careful not to transfer germs from raw meat to cooked meat. Do not carry raw hamburgers to the grill on a platter and then serve cooked meat on the same, unwashed platter.

- You can combine the features of your grill with those of your microwave to speed cooking. Here's a rule of thumb to follow: Foods should be microwaved only *half* of their total microwave time if they are to finish cooking on the grill. Plan preparation time so that foods can go directly from the microwave to the grill. Have coals ready by the time foods are partially microwaved.

SAFETY TIPS

- Don't light any part of the bay containing the briquettes.

- Barbecue away from flammable items such as overhangs and trees.

- Never cover flaming briquettes with a grill lid. This could result in a flare-up when the lid is removed. Use water to control excessive flames.

GRILLED CORN

- 4 ears corn
- 2 T. margarine or butter

Remove large outer husks. Turn back inner husks and remove cornsilk. Spread margarine or butter over corn. Then pull husks back over the ears, tying with fine wire. Cover and grill corn three inches from medium coals. Cook for 15 to 25 minutes, turning frequently, until tender. Remove husks and serve.

BEST BURGERS

- 1½ lb. ground beef
- 1 medium onion, finely chopped
- 1 clove garlic, finely chopped

Brush grill with vegetable oil. Mix onion and garlic into meat. Shape meat mixture into six patties about ¼ inch thick. Grill about four inches from medium coals. Cook four to six minutes on each side, turning once, for medium doneness. Salt and pepper to taste.

COMPREHENSION

Use information from the reading to answer the questions. Write your answers in complete sentences.

1. What are three different kinds of outdoor grills?

_____

2. About how many charcoal briquettes should you use in a standard-size grill?

_____

3. How long does it take to grill corn on the cob?

_____

4. Should the charcoal briquettes be piled up or spread out when you light them?

_____

5. For best results, how close should hamburgers be to the medium-hot coals?

_____

6. What three factors affect cooking times?

_____

SYLLABLES

Say the words from the reading aloud. Then break each word into *syllables* (separate sounds) on the lines below.

thoroughly	sauces	important	briquettes	margarine	fluid

1. _____ / _____   2. _____ / _____ / _____

   _____ / _____   _____ / _____ / _____

   _____ / _____   _____ / _____ / _____

DRAWING CONCLUSIONS

1. Why is it a good idea to use long-handled tools when grilling?

   _____

2. What color are "ashed over" briquettes?

   _____

3. Why does the recipe tell you to brush oil on the grill before barbecuing hamburgers?

   _____

4. What clue might you have that the fire isn't hot enough?

   _____

5. What is one way that germs could be transferred from raw meat to cooked meat?

   _____

   _____

6. What is a *flare-up*? How can it be caused?

   _____

   _____

ANTONYMS

Notice the **boldface** word in each sentence. Then circle a letter to show the *antonym* (word that means the opposite) of the boldface word.

1. Barbecue away from **flammable** items such as trees.

   a. fireproof   b. nearby   c. living

2. Have coals ready by the time foods are **partially** microwaved.

   a. in closed parcels   b. divided into parts   c. completely

3. **Never** cover flaming briquettes with a grill lid.

    a. carefully   b. always   c. under no conditions

4. Use water to control **excessive** flames.

    a. inadequate   b. overwhelming   c. life-threatening

5. Keep your hands a safe distance from **intense** heat.

    a. crucial   b. extreme   c. mild

PUZZLER

Use the clues to help you solve the crossword puzzle. Answers are words that complete the sentences.

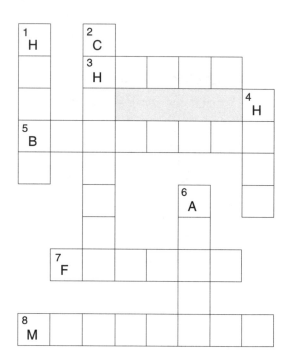

ACROSS

3. Before grilling corn, remove the large outer ___.

5. Apply ___ sauce with a brush before and during cooking.

7. Wood chips add a smoky ___ to grilled foods.

8. Before cooking, meat and fish can be soaked in a flavorful ___.

DOWN

1. Mint and sage are ___ often used for seasoning.

2. Use about 40 ___ briquettes in a standard-size grill.

4. Keep the ___ even throughout the grilling period.

6. Sprinkled over the coals, garlic cloves add flavor and ___.

COMPOUND WORDS

Complete the sentences with compound words from the reading. Combine a word from Box A and a word from Box B to make each compound. Hint: You will use one of the words twice.

```
┌─────────────────BOX A─────────────────┐    ┌───────────────────BOX B───────────────────┐
│   over   fruit   out   summer          │    │   time   wood   door   fill   hang         │
└────────────────────────────────────────┘    └────────────────────────────────────────────┘
```

1. Cooking outdoors was once a special _____ treat.

2. Before tossing on hot coals, soak _____ chips in water for 30 minutes.

3. Do you know how to use an _____ grill safely and skillfully?

4. Do not _____ your grill with briquettes.

5. Flaming coals could set an _____ on fire.

SYNONYMS

Circle the *synonym* (word that means the same) of the **boldface** word in each phrase.

1. **regulate** the heat

   register   adjust   lower

2. **sprinkle** herbs on coals

   dampen   shake   scatter

3. **light** the briquettes

   ignite   illuminate   douse

4. **soak** chips in water

   scrub   steam   immerse

5. dry brush **thoroughly**

   immediately   completely   safely

6. protect from **intense** heat

   direct   flaming   extreme

REVIEW

VOCABULARY

Unscramble the words to complete the sentences.

1. You can microwave fish STILFLE _____ in five to seven minutes.

2. Parsley is often used as a SHINRAG _____ to decorate foods.

3. Wood SPICH _____ add a smoky flavor to grilled foods.

4. Hot or cold foods should not remain at room EMRUTEPRATE _____ for more than two hours.

MULTIPLE CHOICE

Circle a letter to answer each question.

1. Using what device can ensure that meat and poultry are cooked thoroughly?

    a. cutting board   b. food processor   c. meat thermometer

2. Which foods are most perishable?

    a. spices, herbs, and extracts   b. meat, poultry, seafood   c. gravy, casseroles, stews

3. What two effects does marinating have on food?

    a. flavoring and tenderizing   b. reduces sugar and salt   c. blanches and glazes

4. Containers of what shape work best for microwave cooking?

    a. square   b. foam   c. round

BEHIND THE WHEEL

Lesson 1: Fuel Economy

Lesson 2: Defensive Driving

Lesson 3: Equipment Emergencies

Lesson 4: Maintaining Your Car

When you complete this unit, you will be able to answer questions like these:

- *Why is it important to monitor the air pressure in your car's tires?*

- *How can you calculate the number of miles per gallon your car is getting?*

- *If a car accident seems likely, what three things can you do to avoid it?*

- *What should you do if your car's brakes suddenly seem to give out?*

PRETEST

Write **T** or **F** to show whether you think each statement is *true* or *false*.

1. _____ If your gas pedal gets stuck, first shift into neutral gear.

2. _____ The tire pressure gauges at service stations may not always be accurate.

3. _____ To do even simple mechanical jobs, several expensive tools are necessary.

4. _____ At 55 miles per hour, it takes about 800 feet to come to a complete stop.

5. _____ Unnecessary lane changes cause many preventable accidents.

6. _____ Combining several short trips into one saves gasoline.

Pretest answers: 1. T 2. T 3. F 4. F 5. T 6. T

FUEL ECONOMY

Before reading . . .

What can you do to save money on gasoline? Besides buying the least expensive gas you can find, you can avoid wasting gas in several ways. The information in this reading will give you some money-saving tips.

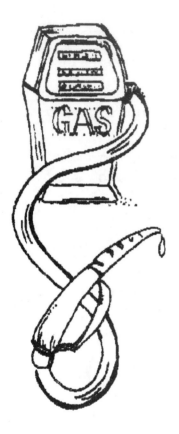

Don't Be a Gas Hog!

- Carefully determine your transportation needs before you buy a car. Choose the size of your vehicle based on normal use and load—not on occasional use. Vehicle weight is a big factor in fuel economy.

- Once you have selected the vehicle that matches your needs, the next choice is the power source. The standard-size engine is generally most efficient. Smaller cars, for example, usually require only a four-cylinder engine.

- Basic convenience equipment reduces fuel economy in two ways: It adds weight and uses engine power. Select only the equipment that is necessary. For example, most small cars do not need power steering.

- Don't buy a car with air conditioning unless it is necessary for a very warm geographic region. Air conditioning will reduce your fuel economy by eight to 16 percent.

- You may pay more for radial tires, but they are cost-efficient. They last longer and perform better on the road.

Calculating Fuel Economy

An estimate of fuel economy tells you *approximately* the distance you can drive for each gallon of fuel that your vehicle uses. Do not try to calculate fuel economy during a new vehicle's break-in period. This would not be an accurate estimate of how much fuel your vehicle will normally use.

To calculate fuel economy:

1. Make sure the fuel tank is full when you record the first odometer reading.

2. Then, every time you buy fuel, fill the tank completely. Write down the number of miles that you have driven and the number of gallons of fuel that you are buying.

   (Keep a record for at least a month. This will give you a more accurate estimate than figuring the fuel economy based on only one or two readings.)

3. Divide the total number of miles that you have driven by the total number of gallons that your vehicle has used.

• EPA fuel economy figures are obtained from laboratory tests under simulated road conditions. These are estimates that may not reflect the actual conditions you experience. The tests also do not exactly duplicate your personal style of driving, including all your stops, starts, and lane changes.

Fuel Conservation

Always try to drive with fuel economy in mind. When you do, you are helping to conserve our valuable energy resources. Driving more efficiently and paying a little more attention to your vehicle's maintenance will quickly become a habit. This habit will help save fuel and reduce car emissions that pollute the air.

Efficiency Counts

Smooth and steady. Drive at a smooth and steady pace. Concentrate and look well ahead of you. When it's safe and legal, steer around problems rather than slowing or stopping.

Combine several short trips. Save unnecessary trips by first trying to locate what you need by phone. During the first mile or two in a cold car, you get only 30–40 percent of the mileage you get when your engine is warm.

MONEY-SAVING DOs AND DON'Ts

If you watch your speed, you'll save money. You can save gas if you drive at a steady, moderate speed. Never coast downhill in neutral gear to save gas. This practice is against the law. Why? Because it is dangerous. Follow these tips:

• Do start off slowly. "Hot rod" driving and quick starts decrease your gas mileage.

• Do hold a steady foot on the gas pedal whenever you can. This can improve your gas mileage by as much as 1.3 miles a gallon. If you stay alert and watch traffic, you can usually avoid having to either suddenly accelerate or stop.

• Don't let the engine idle for a long time.

• Don't carry loads that are too heavy. See your car's owner's manual to find out your vehicle's load limit.

• Do keep the tires properly inflated. This is important for safe vehicle handling as well as for good mileage. Underinflated tires increase fuel consumption.

COMPREHENSION

Write **F** or **O** to show whether each statement is a *fact* or an *opinion*.

1. _____ A car uses more gas when it is cold than it does when it is warmed up.

2. _____ People who drive big, heavy vans are wasteful and selfish.

3. _____ A car that goes 20 miles on a gallon of gas is getting pretty good mileage.

4. _____ It is best to avoid making sudden starts and stops.

5. _____ All gasoline engines pollute the air somewhat.

6. _____ Except in desert regions, automobile air conditioning should be banned.

SENTENCE COMPLETION

First, unscramble the words from the reading. Then use the words to correctly complete the sentences.

LENIDCRY _____	**LEYTS** _____
DRATSNAD _____	**TACROF** _____
MEOTRADE _____	**CHELIVE** _____

1. Proper tire inflation is important for safe _____ handling.

2. Drive at a steady, _____ speed.

3. The _____-size engine is usually most efficient.

4. Road tests don't exactly duplicate your own _____ of driving.

5. Smaller cars usually require only a four-_____ engine.

6. Vehicle weight is a big _____ in fuel economy.

60

PUZZLER

Use words from the reading to complete the crossword puzzle. Answers are words that complete the sentences.

ACROSS

1. Smaller cars don't need _____ steering.

4. Write down the number of _____ of gas you buy.

6. _____ tires are cost-efficient.

7. _____ only additional equipment that is truly necessary.

DOWN

1. Car emissions _____ the air.

2. You use less gas when your _____ is warm.

3. Driving at a _____ speed conserves gasoline.

5. Don't let your car _____ for a long time.

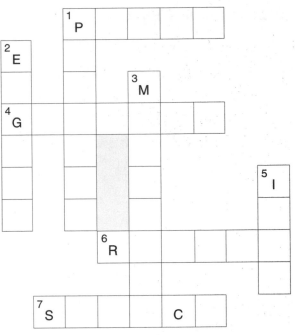

VOCABULARY

Circle a letter to show the meaning of each **boldface** word.

1. Laboratory tests are conducted under **simulated** road conditions.

   a. simple and straightforward
   b. unimaginably difficult
   c. designed to be like the real thing

2. To calculate fuel economy, first record the **odometer** reading.

   a. instrument measuring radiator heat
   b. instrument measuring distance traveled
   c. instrument measuring fuel level

3. Being careful about how you drive helps to **conserve** valuable energy resources.

   a. use wisely
   b. quickly deplete
   c. leave untouched

4. Car **emissions** are a major contributor to smog.

   a. accidents and breakdowns
   b. gridlock on highways
   c. smoke and fumes in exhaust

WORD COMPLETION

Add vowels (*a, e, i, o, u*) to complete the words. The completed sentences give you important advice about calculating fuel economy.

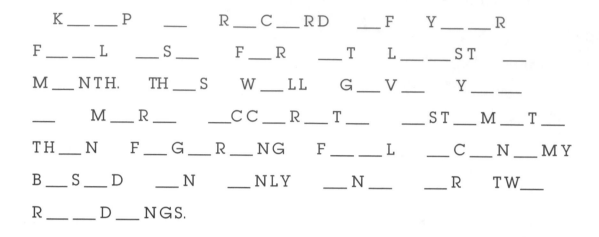

K __ __ P __ R __ C __ RD __ F Y __ __ R

F __ __ L __ S __ F __ R __ T L __ __ ST __

M __ NTH. TH __ S W __ LL G __ V __ Y __ __

__ M __ R __ __ CC __ R __ T __ __ ST __ M __ T __

TH __ N F __ G __ R __ NG F __ __ L __ C __ N __ MY

B __ S __ D __ N __ NLY __ N __ __ R TW __

R __ __ D __ NGS.

PREFIXES: *Over* and *Under*

You read that tires should be inflated properly—not overinflated or underinflated. Knowing that *over* means "too much" and *under* means "too little," complete the words below with **over** or **under**. Use the definitions for clues.

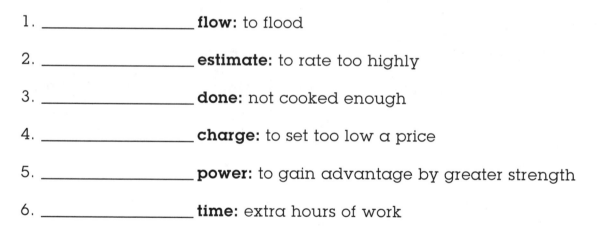

1. _____ **flow:** to flood

2. _____ **estimate:** to rate too highly

3. _____ **done:** not cooked enough

4. _____ **charge:** to set too low a price

5. _____ **power:** to gain advantage by greater strength

6. _____ **time:** extra hours of work

DRAWING CONCLUSIONS FROM DETAILS

Write **T** or **F** to show whether each statement is *true* or *false*.

1. _____ You can get an extra mile on every gallon of gas by driving at a steady rate.

2. _____ To calculate fuel economy, you must figure in the current price for a gallon of gas.

3. _____ Most drivers stop, start, and change lanes in exactly the same way.

4. _____ A "gas hog" is someone who buys premium rather than regular gasoline.

5. _____ Your mileage will increase by about ⅓ when your engine is warm.

6. _____ Lighter weight cars use less gasoline than heavier cars do.

7. _____ CD players are one kind of convenience equipment that reduces mileage.

8. _____ Upgraded equipment that is very expensive could never be considered cost-efficient.

EXAMPLES

Match the examples in the box with the correct headings. Write the examples on the lines. Hint: You will *not* use all the examples.

icy patches	desert	driving to school	heavy traffic
mountains	dead battery	summer vacation	underwater
trip to grocery store		moving to a new apartment	

1. **NORMAL USE**

_____

_____

2. **GEOGRAPHIC REGIONS**

_____

_____

3. **OCCASIONAL USE**

_____

_____

4. **ROAD CONDITIONS**

_____

_____

SYLLABLES

Divide the words *conservation* and *necessary* into syllables (separate sounds).

_____ / _____ / _____ / _____

_____ / _____ / _____ / _____

DEFENSIVE DRIVING

Before reading. . .

What's the best way to protect yourself from auto accidents?
The information in this lesson will help you to stay safe.

What is defensive driving? It is driving to defend yourself against possible accidents caused by bad drivers, drunk drivers, poor weather, and heavy traffic.

You drive defensively when you:

- Look ahead. Look at the side of the road as well as the middle.

- Leave plenty of space between you and the vehicle ahead. This will give you more time to stop or avoid a hazard.

- Keep your eyes moving. Watch for signs warning of problems ahead.

- Leave yourself an "out." Know which lanes are clear so you can use them if you have to.

- Make sure that other drivers see you. Turn on your headlights when visibility is poor.

If you look ahead, and keep your eyes moving, you will spot a hazard more easily. Once you have seen the hazard and decided what to do—you must act. Never "wait and see." Never think that everything will be all right. Children playing in the street may not see you. The boy on the bike may ride in front of you. The man opening a car door in your lane may not see you. If you have an accident, you may not be *legally* at fault. But you may be *morally* at fault, if you could have prevented the accident but didn't. Remember that you can prevent most accidents if you drive defensively.

HOW FAST CAN YOU STOP?

At 55 miles per hour, it takes about 400 feet to bring your car to a complete stop. At 35 miles per hour, it takes about 210 feet to bring your car to a complete stop.

The Most Common Causes of Accidents

- Unsafe speed
- Driving on the wrong side of the road
- Improper turns
- Violation of the right-of-way rules
- Violation of stop signals and signs
- Tailgating (following too closely)
- Inattention
- Rubbernecking
- Unnecessary lane changes

Protecting Yourself in Accidents

To avoid an accident, most drivers hit the brakes first. But sometimes this locks the wheels (unless you have antilock brakes). When a car begins to skid, it makes a dangerous situation worse.

There are three things you can do to avoid an accident. You can stop quickly, turn, or speed up.

- To stop quickly, apply firm, steady pressure on the brake pedal. If the car begins to skid, release the brakes. Then step on the brake pedal again, using firm, steady pressure. Repeat this process until the car stops. Remember that antilock brakes must not be pumped.

- If you don't have time to stop—turn. If you have to, run off the road if there is room. Running off the road is usually better than hitting another car. Try not to brake as you turn.

- Sometimes you can speed up to avoid an accident. This may work if a car is going to hit you on the side or rear.

If you can't avoid an accident, protect yourself as well as you can.

IF YOU ARE GOING TO BE HIT FROM THE REAR:

- Be ready to brake so you won't be pushed into another car.

IF YOU ARE GOING TO BE HIT FROM THE SIDE:

- Brace yourself with the steering wheel. Perhaps you can keep yourself from being thrown against the side of the car.

IF YOU ARE GOING TO BE HIT FROM THE FRONT:

- If you are wearing a shoulder strap, use your arms and hands to protect your face.

- If you are not using a shoulder strap, throw yourself across the seat. This will help you avoid hitting the steering column or the windshield.

> **LOOK BACK AND LEARN**
>
> Have you ever had an accident or a "near miss"? Think about it. Do you know what went wrong? Who made the mistake? Could the accident or near miss have been avoided? It's smart to ask yourself these questions. Perhaps you will see that you need to change your driving habits. Be honest with yourself! Such a change could help you avoid a serious accident later on.

COMPREHENSION

Use information in the reading to help you answer the questions.

1. What five basic things must you do to drive defensively?

   _____

   _____

   _____

   _____

   _____

2. If you're trying to avoid an accident, what problem can be caused by stomping on the brakes?

   _____

3. What should you do if you think your car is about to be hit from the rear?

   _____

4. Why is it a good idea to review your memories of an accident or a "near miss"?

   _____

5. How can most accidents be prevented?

   _____

SYLLABLES

Divide the following words from the reading into syllables (separate sounds).

rubbernecking	column	protecting

1. _____ / _____ /   2. _____ / _____ / _____

3. _____ / _____ / _____ / _____

PUZZLER

Use information in the reading to help you solve the crossword puzzle. Answers are words that complete the sentences.

ACROSS

2. Once you see a _____ ahead, act immediately.

6. You can _____ most accidents if you drive defensively.

7. To avoid being hit, _____ your car off the road.

8. If your car begins to skid, _____ the brakes.

DOWN

1. _____ the braking process until your car stops.

3. _____ driving protects you from avoidable accidents.

4. Apply firm, steady _____ on the brake pedal.

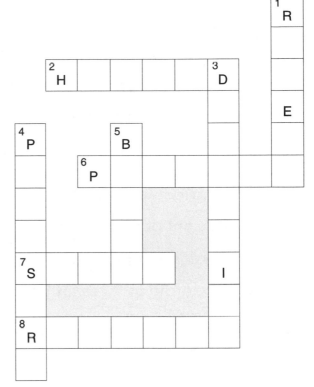

5. _____ yourself against the steering wheel if you are going to be hit from the side.

VOCABULARY

Circle a letter to show the meaning of the **boldface** word or words in each sentence.

1. If you keep your eyes moving, you will be able to spot a **hazard** more easily.

   a. traffic jam   b. police car   c. dangerous situation

2. **Tailgaters** cause innumerable accidents that clog freeways.

   a. drivers of pickup trucks   b. drivers who follow too closely   c. cars with burned out taillights

3. If you **brace** yourself with your steering wheel, you may keep yourself from being thrown against the side of the car.

   a. get ready for a jolt
   b. bend down and crawl under
   c. drive with both hands

4. Violation of **right-of-way** rules causes many needless accidents.

   a. common rules of courtesy practiced by safe drivers

   b. the right to remain silent and call an attorney

   c. legal right to move in front of others in a lane or intersection

5. If the car begins to **skid**, release the brakes.

   a. slide out of control without warning

   b. make jerking movements like skipping and hopping

   c. accelerate to 90 miles per hour

6. Antilock brakes must not be **pumped**.

   a. repeatedly questioned
   b. pressed and released
   c. overinflated

SYNONYMS

Choose a *synonym* (word with the same meaning) from the box for each **boldface** word. Write the word on the line. Hint: You will *not* use all the synonyms in the box.

drivers	perhaps	usually	constant	prevented

1. Step on the brake, using firm, **(steady)** _____ pressure.

2. Many traffic accidents can be **(avoided)** _____.

3. **(Maybe)** _____ you will see that you need to change your driving habits.

4. **(Motorists)** _____ must keep an eye out for children on bikes.

EXAMPLES

Write the examples from the box under the correct headings.

talking on a cell phone	**pouring rain**	**tailgating**
kids playing in the street	**daydreaming**	**heavy traffic**

1.   **BAD DRIVING HABITS**

_____

_____

_____

2.   **DANGEROUS CONDITIONS**

_____

_____

_____

PREFIXES AND SUFFIXES

Use the prefixes and suffixes in the box to complete the **boldface** words.
Hints: (1) You will *not* use all the prefixes and suffixes in the box; (2) In two words, you must double the final consonant before adding the suffix.

pro-	**in-**	**un-**	**re-**	**anti-**	**-ly**	**im-**	**-ing**	**-ed**	**-tion**

1. Many accidents are caused by making _____**proper** turns and driving at an _____**safe** speed.

2. If you have an accident, you may not be **legal**_____ at fault.

3. **Run**_____ off the road is **usual**_____ better than **hit**_____ another car.

4. Ask yourself how the accident could have been **avoid**_____.

5. _____**attention** may cause you to overlook a hazard in the road.

6. Never pump _____**lock** brakes.

7. _____**necessary** lane changes are responsible for many accidents on the highways.

EQUIPMENT EMERGENCIES

Before reading . . .

Vehicles that are very old or poorly maintained can be dangerous. Careful drivers make sure their cars are kept in good working order.

Occasionally, however, you may have to deal with an unexpected equipment problem while you are driving your car. This lesson will help you handle just such a situation.

EQUIPMENT PROBLEMS

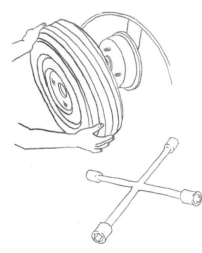

Brake Failure

If your brakes suddenly give out:

- Downshift to low gear.

- Pump the brake pedal fast and hard. This builds up brake fluid pressure. You will know in three to four pumps if the brakes will work. Do not pump antilock brakes.

- Try applying the parking brake. But be ready to release it quickly if the car begins to skid.

- Remember that you can still steer—even if you are swerving! You should try to steer into bushes or something soft.

- To warn other drivers, sound your horn and flash your lights.

- When you no longer need to change direction, turn off the ignition.

Tire Blowout

- Hold the steering wheel tightly and steer straight ahead.

- Slow down gradually. Take your foot off the gas pedal slowly without applying the brakes.

- Once you are off the road, slow to a stop.

- Apply the brakes when the car is almost stopped.

Stuck Gas Pedal

- Shift to neutral gear.
- Apply the brakes.
- Keep your eyes on the road.
- Look for a way out.
- Warn other drivers by blinking and flashing your emergency lights.
- Make every effort to safely drive the car off the road.
- Turn off the ignition when you no longer need to change direction.

Power Steering Failure

If the engine dies:

- Move to the side of the road as safely as possible. You may have to use more force to turn the steering wheel than you normally do.
- Stop the car. If your car has power brakes, you may have to push the brake pedal hard.
- Restart the engine and proceed with caution.

Headlight Failure

If your headlights suddenly go out at night:

- Try the dimmer switch. That will often put them on again.
- Try the headlight switch a few times.
- If that doesn't work, turn on the parking lights, emergency flashers, or turn signals.
- Pull off the road as quickly as possible. Until help arrives, leave the emergency flashers on.

Hood Latch Failure

If your hood suddenly flies up:

- Slow down.
- First, try to see through the windshield by looking under the hood. If you still can't see, try the following:
  - Put your head out the window and look around the hood.
  - Use the center line or the lane marking as a guide.
- Pull off the road as soon as possible. Then, if you have them, turn on your emergency flashers.

When You Are Stuck in Mud or Snow

- Shift to low gear and keep the front wheels straight.
- Gently step on the gas pedal.
- Avoid spinning the wheels. Drive forward as far as possible.
- Shift to reverse and slowly back up as far as possible. Don't spin the wheels.
- Shift to low again and drive forward.
- Repeat this forward-backward rocking motion until the car rolls free.
- Put boards or tree branches under the tires in deep mud or snow. Never do this, however, when the tires are spinning.

COMPREHENSION

Write **T** or **F** to show whether each statement is *true* or *false*. Write **NI** if there is *no information* in the reading to help you make a judgment.

1. _____ Cover your face with your hands just before an airbag is activated.

2. _____ It's best to gun the engine if you're stuck in the mud.

3. _____ Don't apply the brakes if you're slowing down after a tire blowout.

4. _____ If your brakes fail, it might help to apply the parking brake.

5. _____ Steering straight ahead is the only thing you can do if your gas pedal is stuck.

6. _____ It is extremely rare for a hood latch to malfunction.

SPELLING

Circle the correctly spelled word in each group.

1. pedel   peddel   pedal

2. ingine   engine   ingene

3. release   releese   relese

4. swurve   swerve   swerv

5. giude   gide   guide

6. fourward   forewerd   forward

RHYMING WORDS

Choose the word from the box that *rhymes* with each **boldface** word from the reading. Write it on the line. Hint: You will *not* use all the words.

plead	**relied**	**should**	**hook**	**appear**
conceal	**guard**	**rewards**	**buyers**	**spree**

1. **guide** _____

2. **boards** _____

3. **steer** _____

4. **hood** _____

5. **tires** _____

6. **wheel** _____

PUZZLER

Use information from the reading to help you solve the crossword puzzle.
Answers are words that complete the sentences.

ACROSS

2. If the hood blocks your vision, use the lane marking as a _____.

5. If you're stuck in snow, shift to _____ gear.

6. Tires, brakes, and headlights are all part of your car's _____.

7. If your wheels are stuck, _____ step on the gas pedal.

DOWN

1. If your power steering fails, _____ with caution.

2. If your brakes fail, down-shift to low _____.

3. Leave your _____ flashers on until help arrives.

4. If your gas pedal is stuck, shift to _____ gear.

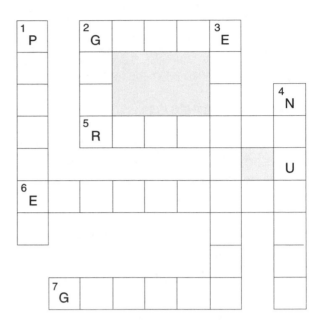

SENTENCE COMPLETION

Unscramble the **boldface** words from the reading to complete the sentences.

1. Your car goes backward when you shift to **SERVERE** _____ gear.

2. Try using the **MIDREM** _____ switch to turn on your headlights.

3. If you have a **TOLOWBU** _____, hold tightly to the steering wheel.

4. **SALEERE** _____ the brakes if your car starts to skid.

5. Warn other drivers by **NILBGINK** _____ your emergency lights.

6. When you no longer need to change **NOCREDITI** _____, turn off the ignition.

PARTS OF SPEECH

Write **N** or **V** to tell whether each **boldface** word is a *noun* or a *verb* as it is used in the sentence. Hint: *Nouns* name persons, places, or things. *Verbs* show action or being.

1. **Shift** (_____) to low gear if your brakes suddenly give out.

2. You can still **steer** (_____) and swerve.

3. You will know in three or four **pumps** (_____) if the brakes will work.

4. Sally works the early **shift** (_____) at the hospital.

5. Take your foot off the gas **pedal** (_____).

6. A **steer** (_____) is a male cow raised for beef.

7. **Pump** (_____) the brake pedal fast and hard.

8. The child is learning to **pedal** (_____) his tricycle.

COMPOUND WORDS

Use a compound word (two or more words combined into one) from the reading to complete each sentence.

1. When you _____, you move the car's transmission to a lower gear.

2. The sudden bursting of a car's tire is called a _____.

3. Turn on your _____ before you start
   to drive at night.

4. If your hood latch springs open, you may not be able to see
   out of the _____.

SYLLABLES

Divide the words from the reading into syllables (separate sounds).

suddenly
situation
direction
unexpected
emergency
dangerous

1. _____ / _____ / _____

   _____ / _____ / _____

   _____ / _____ / _____

2. _____ / _____ / _____ / _____

   _____ / _____ / _____ / _____

   _____ / _____ / _____ / _____

VOCABULARY

Add vowels (a, e, i, o, u) to complete the words from the reading.

1. When a car is in N__ __T R__L, the gears are not meshed
   together. This means they can't transmit power from the engine.

2. The electrical system that starts a car is its __G N__T__ __N. It
   sets fire to the mixture of gases in the cylinders of a gasoline engine.

3. A driver S W__R V__S a car by quickly turning it aside from a
   straight line or path.

4. If you M__ __N T__ __N your car well, you make repairs as soon
   as they are needed.

MAINTAINING YOUR CAR

Before reading . . .

A car is a major investment for most people. It only makes sense to do what you can to protect your investment. This lesson will give you some guidelines for taking good care of your car.

Self-Service Pointers

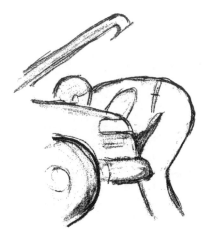

Most drivers pump their own gas. Each time you buy gas, you should also perform a few simple maintenance routines. This extra effort will save you additional money. And even more importantly, it will contribute to the driving efficiency of your vehicle.

The following procedures require only a tire gauge, a rag, an oil can spout, and windshield washer fluid.

- Check the engine oil at every refueling stop.
- Clean the windshield, outside mirrors, and headlights.
- Check the windshield washer fluid.
- Check the tires for excessive worn edges.
- Check the tire pressure at least monthly.

Tire Care Tips

When you check the air pressure in your tires, don't forget to check your spare! Use an accurate tire pressure gauge. Check the tire pressure when the tires are *cold*—after the car has been parked for at least an hour, or when it has been driven for fewer than three miles.

When a tire has *too little pressure*, the outside edges wear out fast. When a tire has *too much air*, it tends to wear out in the middle.

What is the right amount of air? The owner's manual that comes with the car will give you the answer. Often, however, that answer is low. Suppose the book says 24 pounds. That will give you a nice soft ride— but it will also wear out your tires pretty quickly. A better number is 28 pounds. Soft tires give you poor gas mileage.

Some tire gauges in service stations are off as much as eight to ten pounds. It's a good idea to have your own gauge. It won't cost much, and it may save you a lot of money in the long run.

Vehicle Maintenance

Maintain your vehicle *regularly*. A well-tuned, properly maintained vehicle gives you better fuel economy. Follow the recommended schedule in your owner's manual or the one shown below.

Most people have maintenance work done at a service station. The mechanic who works on your car is supposed to check all these things. Then he puts a sticker somewhere on the car. This sticker shows what he did and when he did it. But it is still a good idea to keep an eye on things yourself.

Here is a maintenance schedule that will fit most cars. Ask the mechanic at the service station what different requirements your car may have.

Maintenance Schedule

	LAST SERVICE		NEXT SERVICE	
	DATE	MILEAGE	DATE	MILEAGE
Every 6,000 miles:				
• Change oil and oil filter.	_____	_____	_____	_____
• Grease all fittings.	_____	_____	_____	_____
• Check all fluid levels—power steering pump, brake fluid, transmission, differential, radiator, battery.	_____	_____	_____	_____
• Check tires, hoses and belts.	_____	_____	_____	_____
• Check air filter.	_____	_____	_____	_____
Every 12,000 miles:				
• Tune the engine.	_____	_____	_____	_____
• Check all lightbulbs.	_____	_____	_____	_____
Every 24,000 miles:				
• Repack front wheel bearings.	_____	_____	_____	_____
• Change automatic transmission fluid.	_____	_____	_____	_____
Every two years:				
• Drain and flush radiator.	_____	_____	_____	_____

Some people have learned a good bit about mechanics. They do a lot of routine maintenance work themselves. Not many tools are needed. These people save a lot of money.

COMPREHENSION

Use information from the reading to help you answer the questions.

1. How often should you check the air pressure in your tires?

   _____

2. What parts of your car should you clean every time you buy gas?

   _____

3. How often should you have your car's engine tuned up?

   _____

4. Under what conditions are your tires considered "cold"?

   _____

   _____

5. Why might it be a good idea to buy your own tire pressure gauge?

   _____

6. It's a good idea to check your windshield washer fluid every time
   you stop for gas. What other fluid level should you check that often?

   _____

INFERENCE

To **tune up** your car's engine means to adjust its parts so it will work better.
Cross out the automotive services that would *not* be included in a tune-up. If
you need help with unfamiliar words, check a dictionary.

- clean spark plugs
- repair radio
- repair hubcap
- change oil filter
- charge battery
- clean carburetor

PUZZLER

Use the clues to help you solve the crossword puzzle. Answers are words from the reading that complete the sentences.

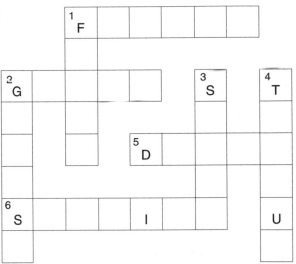

ACROSS

1. Change your oil _____ every 6,000 miles.

2. Use an accurate tire pressure _____.

5. _____ and flush your radiator every two years.

6. Most people have their cars maintained at a _____ station.

DOWN

1. Check your transmission _____ every 6,000 miles.

2. _____ all fittings.

3. Don't forget to check the air pressure in your _____ tire.

4. _____ the engine every 12,000 miles.

RHYMING

Circle the word that *rhymes* with each **boldface** word from the reading.

1. an oil can **spout**   spurt   spot   doubt   cloud

2. check the **hoses**   horses   dozes   hosts   closest

3. **front** wheel bearings   blunt   flaunt   mount   frowned

4. check your **spare**   spear   spar   clear   tear

SPELLING

Circle the correct spelling of each word from the reading.

1. preform   perform   purform   3. gauge   guage   gage

2. presure   preshure   pressure   4. milege   mileage   milage

SYLLABLES

Divide the words from the reading into syllables (separate sounds).

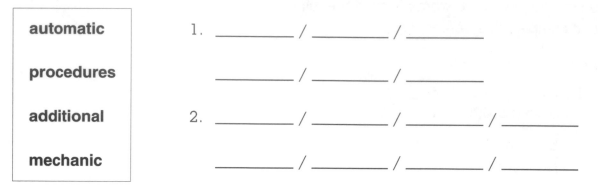

automatic	1. _____ / _____ / _____
procedures	_____ / _____ / _____
additional	2. _____ / _____ / _____ / _____
mechanic	_____ / _____ / _____ / _____

SYNONYMS

Find a *synonym* (word that means the same or nearly the same) in the box for each **boldface** word from the reading. Write the synonyms on the lines. Hint: You will *not* use all the words in the box.

trade	replace	optional	unnecessary
extra	repair	examine	required

1. Not many tools are **needed** to do simple
   mechanical jobs.   _____

2. **Change** engine oil every 6,000 miles.   _____

3. Check the air pressure in your **spare** tire. _____

4. Be sure to **check** your hoses and belts.   _____

VOCABULARY

Circle a letter to show the meaning of each **boldface** word as it is used in the sentence.

1. Be sure to use an accurate tire pressure **gauge**.

   a. compartment for holding fluid
   b. loudly beeping warning system
   c. device for measuring something

2. Drivers can learn to perform a few simple maintenance **routines**.

   a. very boring tasks
   b. dance steps
   c. methods of doing something

3. The owner's **manual** is usually kept in the glove compartment.

   a. small book of instructions
   b. collection of warranties and guarantees
   c. handy, all-purpose tool

4. Regular tune-ups ensure that your engine runs **efficiently**.

   a. at maximum capacity
   b. smoothly and effectively
   c. on very little gasoline

SUFFIXES

Notice the **boldface** words from the reading. Then rewrite the word, adding a suffix from the box, to correctly complete each sentence. Hint: You will *not* use all the suffixes in the box.

-al	**-ly**	**-ing**	**-age**	**-ance**	**-ence**

1. Doing your own simple **(maintain)** _____ procedures can save a lot of money.

2. Tires that are too soft give you poor gas **(mile)** _____.

3. Don't forget to check your power **(steer)** _____ fluid.

4. Check your tires for **(excessive)** _____ worn edges.

ALPHABETICAL ORDER

Renumber the words from the reading to show *alphabetical order.* The first one has been done for you.

1. _____ transmission

2. _____ brakes

3. _____ engine

4. _____ windshield

5. _____ tires

6. _____ radiator

7. _____ wheels

8. _1_ battery

9. _____ hoses

10. _____ belts

SENTENCE COMPLETION

Complete the sentences with words from the lesson.

1. _____ tires last longer and perform better on the road.

2. If you spot a _____ ahead, decide what to do and act immediately.

3. Never _____ antilock brakes.

4. Most people have their cars maintained by a _____ at a service station.

5. Air conditioning _____ fuel economy by 8 to 16 percent.

6. Leave plenty of _____ between your car and the vehicle just ahead.

7. The edges of _____ tires wear out too quickly.

8. If your brakes fail, first _____ to low gear.

SYNONYMS

Draw a line to match each word on the left with its synonym (word with the same meaning) on the right.

1. **estimate**   surprising

2. **calculate**   plan

3. **unexpected**   defend

4. **protect**   manage

5. **conserve**   guess

6. **schedule**   figure

IT'S THE LAW!

When you complete this unit, you will be able to answer questions like these:

- *If you buy online, what's the number-one scam to watch out for?*

- *Under what circumstances are traffic tickets dismissed by a judge?*

- *What steps must you take to sue someone in small-claims court?*

- *What civil rights are guaranteed by the 14th Amendment to the U.S. Constitution?*

PRETEST

Write **T** or **F** to show whether you think each statement is *true* or *false*.

1. _____ An employer cannot deny a worker a promotion on the basis of race, color, sex, age, or national origin.

2. _____ Small-claims court trials are held in a judge's office rather than in a courtroom.

3. _____ If a telemarketer's offer sounds too good to be true, it probably is.

4. _____ If you have too many moving violations, you can lose your driver's license.

5. _____ It's a mistake to send cash when you're ordering a product by mail.

6. _____ If you receive unordered merchandise, you must always return it immediately.

Pretest answers: 1. T 2. F 3. T 4. T 5. T 6. F

LET THE BUYER BEWARE!

Before reading . . .

Potential buyers are always at risk in the marketplace. In ancient Rome, the expression, "*Caveat emptor!*" was used as a warning to consumers. This is still good advice. Translated from Latin, it means, "Let the buyer beware!"

Avoiding Pitfalls in the Marketplace

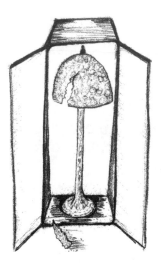

Numerous federal, state, and local laws protect your rights as a consumer. These laws have been greatly strengthened over the past 20 years. But there are two protections that consumers must supply for themselves: common sense and a reasonable amount of knowledge.

Think before making a purchase or entering into an agreement with a merchant.

An informed consumer . . .

- asks questions.
- reads the fine print.
- keeps careful records.
- knows his or her rights.
- protests illegal treatment.
- consults an attorney, if necessary.

TIP: WEB SCAMS

Online auctions have become popular—with eager buyers and crooked dealers alike! That's why online auctions recently topped the National Consumer League's list of the Top 10 Internet Scams.

Rounding out the list, in order, are:

- General merchandise sales
- Internet access services
- Computer equipment and software
- Work-at-home schemes
- Magazine sales
- Travel/Vacation offers
- Multilevel marketing and pyramid schemes
- Collectibles/antiques/memorabilia

Most of the items listed are also common telemarketing scams—with one important distinction.

"Most telemarketing scams involve false promises to make, win, or borrow money," says the NCL's Susan Grant. In contrast, most victims of Internet scams report a different kind of fraud. These are people who bought merchandise that either never arrived or was different from what they had expected.

As always, "buyer beware" is the best strategy. Wise buyers use extreme caution when doing business with unfamiliar companies or dealers. Smart shoppers pay with a credit card whenever possible. This practice makes it much easier to dispute the charges in cases of nondelivery or misrepresentation.

Mail-Order Purchases

Before buying by mail, compare different offers. Then think about the exaggerated wording used in most advertising claims. Would you be willing to accept a product that was *slightly* less wonderful than described? Finally, check to see if the catalog offers a money-back warranty. If so, you will be able to return the product if you are dissatisfied with it.

Then, if you decide to order by mail, be sure to do the following:

• Keep a copy of the ad or catalog from which you ordered.

• Check the time limit on delivery. If the product doesn't arrive as promised, cancel the order by letter.

• Do not send cash. Pay the correct amount (including extra charges such as shipping, handling, sales tax) by check.

• When you receive your order, check it immediately. If it is broken—or not what you ordered—return it to the sender. Then notify the company in writing and keep a copy of your letter.

Unordered Merchandise

Merchants who send unordered merchandise violate the Federal Trade Commission Act. *You do not have to pay for anything you didn't order.* In most states, you don't even have to return unordered merchandise.

Telephone Sales

Telemarketers are clever. Some solicit business, for example, by telling you that you've won a prize. Then they tell you where to go to pick up your prize. But they *don't* tell you about the substantial "transfer fee" you must pay to actually take home what you have "won"!

Here is some good advice regarding telephone solicitations:

• If the deal seems too good to be true, it probably is.

• Never give your credit card number to a stranger on the telephone.

• Before investing money, ask to see a written prospectus.

• Review the written prospectus carefully and show it to your lawyer.

• Follow your lawyer's advice. Don't invest money in a telephone solicitation against legal advice.

COMPREHENSION

Circle the word or words that correctly complete each sentence.

1. (Inline / Online) auctions top the list of Internet scams.

2. In the past two decades, laws protecting consumers have been
   (weakened / strengthened).

3. The consumer's best (strategy / solicitation) is "buyer beware."

4. If a product you've ordered arrives in poor condition, you should
   (return it to the sender / call the Federal Trade Commission.)

5. Informed consumers are not ignorant of their (claims / rights).

6. (Uninsured / Unordered) merchandise usually doesn't even
   have to be returned.

INFERENCE

Think about the reasons *behind* some of the statements in the reading.
Then answer the questions in complete sentences.

1. Why do you think smart consumers keep careful records?

   _____

   _____

2. Why might a company send people products they never ordered?

   _____

3. What warning about telemarketing deals is a general statement
   of "common sense"?

   _____

PUZZLER

Use information in the reading to help you solve the crossword puzzle.
Answers are words that complete the sentences.

ACROSS

4. When you order by mail, keep a copy of the ____.

6. Federal, state, and local laws protect your rights as a ____.

7. ____ auctions are the number one Internet scam.

8. If you are sent the wrong item, ____ it immediately.

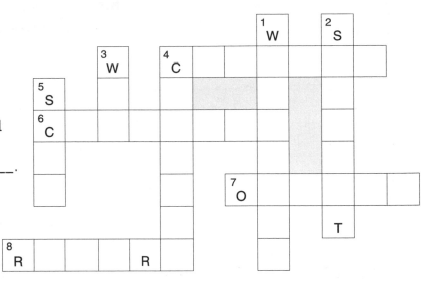

DOWN

1. See if the catalog offers a money-back ____.

2. Some telemarketers use tricks to ____ business.

3. A telemarketer might tell you that you've ____ a prize.

4. Use ____ when dealing with an unfamiliar company.

5. An offer to make a big profit working at home is probably a ____.

SYNONYMS

First, unscramble the words from the reading. Then write each unscrambled word next to its *synonym* (word with the same meaning).

MACS _____	**NIROFDEM** _____
REDALE _____	**SCEONURM** _____
PYCO _____	**WYREAL** _____

1. knowledgeable: _____
2. swindle: _____
3. seller: _____

4. duplicate: _____
5. attorney: _____
6. buyer: _____

ALPHABETICAL ORDER

List the words from the reading in alphabetical order.

violate	auction	prospectus	distinction	merchandise
consult	strategy	eager	substantial	victims

1. _____

2. _____

3. _____

4. _____

5. _____

6. _____

7. _____

8. _____

9. _____

10. _____

SPELLING

Circle the correctly spelled word in each group.

1. knowlege
   knowledge
   knowlidge

2. warrenty
   warranty
   warantee

3. exagerated
   exxagerated
   exaggerated

4. stratagy
   stratigy
   strategy

5. scheme
   scheem
   scheame

6. auctions
   awktions
   aucsions

FACT AND OPINION

Write **F** or **O** to show whether each statement below is a *fact* or an *opinion.*

1. _____ Only a fool would buy an expensive product sight unseen.

2. _____ It is best not to risk giving your credit card number to a stranger on the telephone.

3. _____ Most telemarketing scams have to do with making, borrowing, or winning money.

4. _____ Credit card purchases are easier to cancel than cash purchases.

5. _____ Constant calls from telemarketers are a nuisance; all telemarketing should be against the law.

6. _____ A sales pitch, whether it be in person, on the Internet, or by telephone, is called a *solicitation*.

VOCABULARY

Circle a letter to show the meaning of the **boldface** words from the reading.

1. The expression, **"Caveat emptor!"** was often used in ancient Rome.

   a. bearer of the emperor
   b. try to buy low and sell high
   c. let the buyer beware

2. Review a company's **prospectus** before investing money.

   a. written statement of a new business's main features

   b. something good that is expected to happen soon

   c. set of laws that govern all new business ventures

3. There's an important **distinction** between telemarketing and Internet scams.

   a. confusion
   b. difference
   c. exaggeration

4. Not all dealers on the Internet or on the telephone are engaged in **fraud**.

   a. deliberately making dishonest claims

   b. selling the highest-quality goods

   c. shipping out unordered merchandise

SYLLABLES

Divide each word from the reading into *syllables* (separate sounds).

violate	victims	potential	notify	supply	advice	Internet

1. _____ / _____   _____ / _____   _____ / _____

2. _____ / _____ / _____   _____ / _____ / _____

   _____ / _____ / _____   _____ / _____ / _____

TRAFFIC VIOLATIONS

Before reading . . .

Even careful drivers are sometimes ticketed for traffic violations. How you handle the situation can make the difference between major trouble and a minor inconvenience.

Driving rules and violations are governed by state, county, and local laws. In general, there are two kinds of driving violations.

Routine and Serious Infractions

Tickets are given for routine infractions. These minor violations include such things as illegally parking in front of a fire hydrant or allowing the meter to expire when your car is parked. More serious violations occur when your car is moving. Speeding and failing to stop at a red light or a stop sign are examples of moving violations.

Routine violations usually result in small fines—usually, not more than $50. Such infractions rarely count as points against a driver's record. Serious moving violations, however, can be considered criminal misdemeanors. Under the laws of many states, such violations can result in suspension or revocation of a driver's license. Monetary fines for violations such as reckless driving are often imposed. And sometimes there are additional penalties such as attending driving school, jail time—or a combination of both for serious offenders.

What to Do When You Receive a Ticket

Examine the ticket carefully. The ticket should list the make, model, and body type of your car. It should also list the date your auto registration expires, the violation you are charged with, and the date, time, and place where the alleged violation occurred.

Be sure the information on the ticket is legible and complete. If it is not, you may want to plead not guilty. To do that you must appear in traffic court to fight the ticket. In some states, incomplete or illegible tickets are automatically dismissed at the driver's request. That's why you should never throw away an improperly written ticket.

If You Are Involved in an Accident . . .

- You must stop. Someone could be injured and need your help. If you fail to stop, you may be **charged** with "hit and run." Conviction for this offense carries severe punishment.

- If anyone appears to be hurt, call the police or highway patrol immediately.

- The other driver or person involved will want to see your driver's license, auto registration slip, current address, and evidence of insurance. Have this information ready for the other person as well as the peace officer.

- If you hit a parked vehicle or other property, try to find the owner. If you can't find the owner, leave a note with your name, address, and telephone number. Report the accident immediately to the local police or the highway patrol.

- If you injure or kill an animal, pull over to the side of the road and stop. If you can't find the owner, call the police or the nearest humane society. Do not try to move an injured animal. Never leave an injured animal to die without calling for help.

TRAFFIC TICKET DON'TS

Suppose you are given a traffic ticket for a serious violation. To avoid committing other crimes, remember the following rules:

- If you are signaled to pull over, don't try to evade the police officer.

- Don't argue with the police officer or use threatening language.

- Don't refuse to show your driver's license, insurance information, or registration slip.

- Don't drive away from the scene before the ticket is given to you.

- Don't refuse to take a breathalyzer or drug test if requested.

- If you can help it, don't incriminate yourself by admitting guilt.

COMPREHENSION

Write **T** or **F** if the statement is *true* or *false*. Write **NI** if there is *no information* in the reading to help you make a judgment.

1. _____ Reckless driving is considered a routine infraction.

2. _____ You may lose your driver's license if you are convicted of too many moving violations.

3. _____ If no one sees you hit a parked car, you don't have to report it.

4. _____ Driving under the influence of alcohol or drugs is always punishable by time in prison.

5. _____ Parking next to a fire hydrant is a serious criminal misdemeanor.

6. _____ A judge may dismiss a traffic ticket that is impossible to read.

FORMS OF A WORD

Circle one word in each group that is *not* a different form of the **boldface** word from the reading.

1. **violation**   violate   violence   violator

2. **revocation**   revoke   revoking   revolting

3. **admitting**   administering   admission   admit

4. **registration**   register   registry   regress

SYNONYMS

Draw a line to connect each word from the reading on the left with its *synonym* (word with the same meaning) on the right.

1. **severe**   study

2. **evidence**   unproven

3. **alleged**   readable

4. **legible**   proof

5. **examine**   harsh

6. **infraction**   violation

ANTONYMS

First, unscramble the words in the box. Then write each word next to its *antonym* (word that means the opposite) below.

LITGUY _____   **IROSEUS** _____

EARRYL _____   **DIMAT** _____

JURINED _____   **ALNEPSITE** _____

---

1. healed: _____   4. rewards: _____

2. usually: _____   5. deny: _____

3. minor: _____   6. innocent: _____

PUZZLER

Use the clues to help you solve the crossword puzzle. Answers are words that complete the sentences.

ACROSS

1. Never try to move an injured _____.

6. If you hit a parked _____, try to find the owner.

8. Don't drive away from the _____ before the ticket is given to you.

DOWN

2. Illegal parking is not a _____ violation.

3. A judge may dismiss a charge if the _____ is illegible.

4. Never _____ to take a breathalyzer test.

5. Many _____ revoke licenses for criminal misdemeanors.

7. The _____ society will pick up an injured animal.

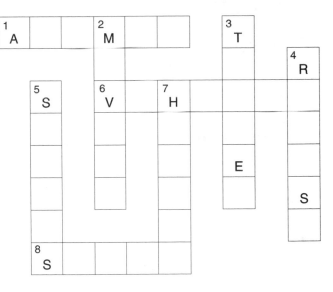

93

SPELLING

Circle the correctly spelled word in each group.

1. liesence
   lisence
   license

2. offenders
   offendors
   ofennders

3. plead
   pleed
   plede

4. enfractions
   infractions
   infracsions

5. rutine
   routine
   rootine

6. patrole
   patroll
   patrol

7. current
   currante
   courent

8. metor
   meeter
   meter

SYLLABLES

Divide the words from the reading into *syllables* (separate sounds).

misdemeanor	1. _____ / _____ / _____
infraction	_____ / _____ / _____
illegible	_____ / _____ / _____
accident	2. _____ / _____ / _____ / _____
information	_____ / _____ / _____ / _____
evidence	_____ / _____ / _____ / _____

VOCABULARY

Circle a letter to show the meaning of the **boldface** word or words.

1. Never try to **evade** a police officer.

   a. avoid, dodge   b. scold, lecture   c. enrage, madden

2. Don't **incriminate** yourself if you don't have to.

   a. say inconsistent   b. try to make   c. act or look
      things   excuses   guilty

3. On what date does your auto registration **expire**?

    a. renew; begin   b. go out   c. require
       again   of date   payment

4. If you are convicted of causing a **"hit and run"** accident, you
will be severely punished.

    a. colliding with   b. hitting someone   c. fleeing the scene
       a runner   with your fists   of an accident

5. **Monetary** fines are often imposed for serious moving violations.

    a. hard labor or   b. having to do   c. time in jail
       community service   with money   or prison

PREFIXES

You know that prefixes are groups of letters added at the beginning of words to change their meaning. To correctly complete each sentence, add a prefix from the box to each **boldface** word. Hint: You will use one prefix more than once.

| Il- | im- | in- | un- |

1. Never throw away an _____**properly** written ticket.

2. It is _____**legal** to fail to stop at a red light.

3. An _____**complete** traffic ticket may be dismissed at the

    driver's request.

4. Speeding is _____**lawful** in every city and state.

5. By law, a police officer's handwriting on a ticket must not be

    _____**legible**.

SMALL-CLAIMS COURT

> **Before reading . . .**
>
> Suppose a neighbor's dog damages your property, and your neighbor refuses to pay for repairs. Would you have to hire a lawyer? Small-claims courts hear more than one million cases a year in the United States. This lesson gives you basic information about small-claims courts and how they operate.

Small-claims courts work. Matters are resolved quickly—sometimes within a month of the filing date. What is the maximum of money you can recover in a small-claims court? The amount varies from state to state, but it is usually up to $3,500.

Do You Have a Claim?

Before you sue anyone for damages, make sure you have a valid claim. In order to be successful, you must be able to:

- identify the person or business that damaged or caused you harm;

- calculate the amount of damages you have suffered;

- show that there is some basis in law to have a court award you damages;

- show that you were not the main cause of your own harm.

Not all damages or losses are recoverable. Suppose, for example, that someone hit you and cut your face. You hope to collect $150 to pay the doctor for stitching the cut. But suppose the other person's witnesses testify that *you* threw the first blow. In that case, your claim is not likely to be considered valid.

Starting the Lawsuit

You begin the lawsuit by paying a small fee (usually about $5). Then you must go to court in person or mail in a complaint. The complaint must state the following information:

- your name and address
- the complete name and address of the person, business, or company you are suing
- the amount of money you believe you are owed
- the facts of your case
- the reasons you (the plaintiff) are seeking redress

Before the Trial

Preparation is important. Gather and label all your evidence ahead of time. Examples of essential documents might include:

- receipts and canceled checks
- clear photographs of damaged property
- an employer's statement of lost wages
- medical bills and reports
- police and accident reports
- actual exhibits, if possible (such as the used part that was installed in your car instead of the new part you paid for)
- estimates for repair or replacement

At the Trial

Arrive early, locate the correct courtroom, and check in with the clerk. Wearing business clothes shows respect for the court.

After you and your opponent are sworn in, the judge will conduct the hearing and ask you questions. Then your opponent will make a statement. Do not interrupt your opponent's presentation. Be diplomatic rather than emotional. After your opponent has finished speaking, you will have a chance to point out any flaws in his or her side of the story.

Obtaining Judgment

Some small-claims court judges render an oral opinion on the spot. Others issue a written decision several days after the hearing. This gives them time to weigh the testimony and the exhibits. If your opponent failed to attend the hearing, a judge usually renders a judgment of default. This decides the case in favor of the plaintiff.

Don't hesitate to act if you don't receive the money you are awarded. A law enforcement officer has the power to go out and collect a judgment. The clerk of your small-claims court will be able to tell you exactly what to do.

COMPREHENSION

Write **T** or **F** if the statement is *true* or *false*. Write **NI** if there is *no information* in the reading to help you make a judgment.

1. _____ Judges in small-claims courts sometimes award vast amounts of money for pain and suffering.

2. _____ You might go to small-claims court to sue a dry cleaner for losing your best suit.

3. _____ Small-claims courts in this country handle more one million cases every year.

4. _____ If you take a lawyer with you, you have a better chance of winning a small-claims case.

5. _____ Important documents to take to court include your Social Security card and your driver's license.

6. _____ Clerks in small-claims courts are usually sympathetic to defendants.

SYNONYMS

First, unscramble the words from the reading. Then write each unscrambled word next to its *synonym* (word with the same meaning.)

COTALE _____	SEGWA _____
NERDER _____	WERPO _____
REPORTYP _____	RAVESI _____

1. authority: _____   4. earnings: _____

2. find: _____   5. deliver: _____

3. possessions: _____   6. differs: _____

PUZZLER

Use information in the reading to help you complete the crossword puzzle. Answers are words that complete the sentences.

ACROSS

2. The amount of money you can recover ___ from state to state.

3. Your written ___ must include the facts of the case.

5. You don't need a lawyer to ___ for damages in small-claims court.

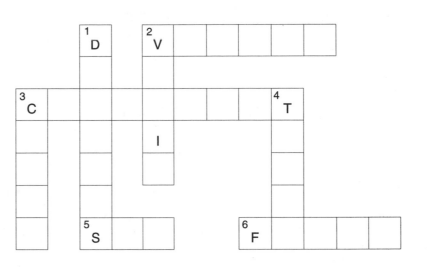

6. You will have a chance to point out ___ in your opponent's side of the story.

DOWN

1. Not all ___ or losses are recoverable.

2. Before you sue, make sure that your claim is ___.

3. The court ___ will tell you how to collect your award.

4. Wear business clothes on the day of the ___.

NOTING DETAILS

1. About how much is the fee for filing a complaint in small-claims court? _____

2. What's the maximum amount of money awarded in most small-claims courts? _____

3. What usually happens if the defendant fails to appear in small-claims court? _____

   _____

4. Who speaks first in a small-claims trial—
   the plaintiff or the defendant? _____

SPELLING

Circle the correctly spelled word in each group.

1.	2.	3.	4.
reciepts	interupt	estimates	propperty
receets	interuppt	estamates	property
receipts	interrupt	estemates	proparty

SYLLABLES

Divide each word from the reading into *syllables* (separate sounds).

installed	resolved	calculate	opponent	hesitate	trial	exactly

1. _____ / _____   _____ / _____   _____ / _____

2. _____ / _____ / _____   _____ / _____ / _____

   _____ / _____ / _____   _____ / _____ / _____

VOCABULARY

Circle a letter to show the meaning of the **boldface** word or words.

1. When you appear in court, be **diplomatic** rather than emotional.

   a. bring your diploma with you   b. dress like an important diplomat   c. calm, tactful, courteous

2. Some judges want several days to **weigh** the testimony and exhibits.

   a. carefully
      consider

   b. verify or
      confirm

   c. dispute or
      disprove

3. A law enforcement officer may be assigned to collect the **judgment**.

   a. court papers

   b. money you are owed

   c. judge's garment

4. If you caused your own harm, your claim will not be **valid**.

   a. truthful

   b. have legal force

   c. valueless

5. Your complaint must give your reasons for seeking **redress**.

   a. correction for
      a wrong done

   b. a brand
      new outfit

   c. time to change
      clothes

6. Gather and label all your **evidence** before the trial.

   a. opening
      statements

   b. books from the
      law library

   c. proofs of
      what happened

ALPHABETICAL ORDER

List the words from the reading in alphabetical order.

| sworn | courtroom | testimony | identify | opponent |
| decision | report | lawsuit | hearing | photograph |

1. _____

2. _____

3. _____

4. _____

5. _____

6. _____

7. _____

8. _____

9. _____

10. _____

EQUAL PROTECTION

Before reading . . .

Equal protection under the law is the right of every American. Fair treatment for all is guaranteed by the United States Constitution. This lesson discusses "equal protection" and offers strategies for exercising your rights.

Each citizen of the United States has the same rights and obligations as any other. Federal, state, and local governments prohibit bias. One group of people or an individual may not be favored over another on the basis of age, color, national origin, race, or sex.

The right to equal protection applies to all areas. This includes employment and education as well as public accommodations and housing.

The following prohibitions apply, for example, to government agencies, employers, and labor unions, as well as to other organizations.

Race, color, national origin, sex, or age may *not* be the basis for:

- **denying an applicant a job.**

- **denying promotions, transfers, or assignments.**

- **penalizing workers by reducing privileges, employment opportunities, or compensation.**

- **firing a worker.**

If you have been treated unfairly on the job, act quickly. Speak to an attorney or to your state's Commission on Human Rights as soon as possible. Complaints must be filed within a certain time limit. If you wait too long to file, the statute of limitations may apply.

IT'S AGAINST THE LAW!

People cannot be refused service by a public restaurant or other retail establishment on the basis of sex, race, color, or national origin. Private facilities, however (such as a men's club supported by private members' dues) can generally exclude women or members of other groups.

No one can legally stop you from filing a complaint. You cannot be fired because you are protesting illegal treatment. The law forbids employers from threatening reprisals or retaliation.

Suppose your case comes to court.

Here are some things you can do to increase your chances of winning a discrimination case:

- **Speak to other minority employees.** Find out if they have received similar discriminatory treatment.

- **Discuss the problem with friendly witnesses.** Ask if they are willing to testify on your behalf to help you prove your claim.

- **Put your complaint in writing.** Suppose you receive an unfavorable performance review that you feel is unjustified. Submit a written response that documents why the appraisal is incorrect.

> The *14th Amendment to the Constitution* says that the states may not deny people their right to *equal opportunity.* State and local laws support federal laws against discrimination.
>
> The laws do *not* say that everyone must be treated exactly the same way in every case. But the laws *do* say that no one can be treated unfairly. All people are guaranteed equal opportunity. That means they must receive the same chance as everyone else to do something or have something.

COMPREHENSION

Write **T** or **F** if a statement is *true* or *false.* Write **NI** if there is *no information* in the reading to help you make a judgment.

1. _____ To fire a minority worker for any reason is always against the law.

2. _____ The right to equal protection extends beyond the workplace to education and housing.

3. _____ A great number of citizens objected when the 14th Amendment was added to the Constitution.

4. _____ Public restaurants are not allowed to deny service to anyone for *any* reason.

PREFIXES

You know that *prefixes* are groups of letters added at the beginning of words to change their meaning. The prefixes *il-*, *in-*, and *un-* mean "not." Add one of these prefixes to each word below. Check a dictionary if you're not sure.

1. _____ correct

2. _____ legal

3. _____ lawful

4. _____ justified

5. _____ action

6. _____ fair

7. _____ accurate

8. _____ literate

9. _____ complete

10. _____ legible

SUFFIXES

You know that *suffixes* are groups of letters added at the end of words to change their meaning. Rewrite each **boldface** word, adding the correct suffix from the box. Hint: You will *not* use all the suffixes.

-ent	-ant	-ions	-er	-al	-ment	-ing

1. A retail **(establish)** _____ cannot deny service on the basis of race, color, sex, or national origin.

2. An **(employ)** _____ cannot fire you for protesting illegal treatment.

3. **(Nation)** _____ origin is an illegal reason for denying someone a promotion.

4. Several **(prohibit)** _____ apply to employers and labor unions.

5. An **(apply)** _____ cannot be denied a job on the basis of sex or age.

PUZZLER

Use information in the reading to help you complete the crossword puzzle. Answers are words that complete the sentences.

ACROSS

2. An _____ cannot be denied a job because of color.

4. Federal, state, and local laws _____ discrimination.

6. If you have been treated unfairly, speak to an _____.

DOWN

1. Speak to other _____ employees.

2. The 14th _____ guarantees equal opportunity.

3. Ask witnesses if they will _____ for you in court.

5. Discrimination on the _____ of age, sex, national origin, race, or color is forbidden.

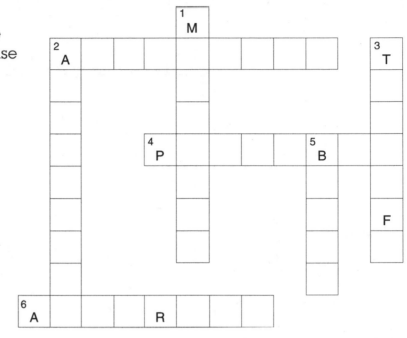

CONTEXT CLUES

Use *context clues* to figure out the meaning of the **boldface** word or words. Circle a letter to show your answer.

1. If you wait too long to file a claim, the **statute of limitations** may apply.

   a. requirement to begin a lawsuit within a certain time period

   b. law that forbids court cases from lasting too long

   c. law that grants lawyers enough time to prepare a case

2. Ask friendly witnesses if they will testify **on your behalf**.

   a. for only half the trial
   b. to help you prove your case
   c. sit right beside you

3. Suppose you receive an unfavorable **performance review** that you think is unjustified.

   a. harsh scolding for a big mistake you made

   b. unkind or rude treatment from fellow workers

   c. an employer's formal evaluation of your work

4. Consult an experienced **labor lawyer** before taking any action on your own.

   a. attorney who shares the work with you

   b. attorney who specializes in workplace law

   c. lawyer who works extremely hard

SPELLING

Circle the correctly spelled word in each group.

1. priviledge	2. accommodations	3. restarant	4. indavidual
privelege	accomodations	restaurant	individuel
privilege	acommodations	restaraunt	individual

VERB OR NOUN?

The same word can be a different part of speech, depending upon how it is used in a sentence. You know that *nouns* name persons, places, and things. *Verbs* are words that show action or state of being. Read each sentence below. Decide whether each **boldface** word is used as a noun or a verb. Write **N** or **V** on the line.

1. _____ A written response **documents** why you think the appraisal is unfair.

2. _____ Did you **witness** any acts of discrimination?

3. _____ Bring all of your **documents** with you to court.

4. _____ Ask a friendly **witness** to testify for you.

PLURALS

Write the *plural* form (names more than one) of each word from the reading.
Check a dictionary if you're not sure.

1. one **minority**,

   two _____

2. one **attorney**,

   two _____

3. one **facility**,

   two _____

4. one **opportunity**,

   two _____

STATING OPINIONS

Write your answers in complete sentences.

1. Do you think it was necessary to add the 14th Amendment to the
   Constitution? Explain your reasoning.

   _____

   _____

2. Do you think anti-discrimination laws have eliminated unfairness in
   the workplace? If you can, support your opinion with examples.

   _____

   _____

VOCABULARY

Write a letter to match each word on the left with its meaning on the right. Use
context clues in the reading for help.

1. _____ **prohibit**

2. _____ **compensation**

3. _____ **bias**

4. _____ **appraisal**

5. _____ **version**

6. _____ **retaliate**

a. to strike back by harming someone who has harmed you

b. judgment of the worth of something or someone

c. report from one person's point of view

d. wages or other payment for work

e. prejudice in favor of or against something

f. to forbid by law

— **REVIEW** —

VOCABULARY

Unscramble the words to complete the sentences.

1. The National Consumer League warns shoppers to watch out for different kinds of **RUDAF** _____.

2. Serious moving violations are considered **RAINMICL** _____ misdemeanors.

3. In small-claims court, you can recover **MADSAGE** _____ up to $3,500.

4. You cannot be **DRIFE** _____ for protesting unfair treatment in the workplace.

MULTIPLE CHOICE

Circle a letter to answer each question.

1. What are two protections that consumers must supply for themselves?

   a. thrift and suspicion
   b. common sense and knowledge
   c. cash and credit cards

2. What must you do if you hit a parked car and can't find the owner?

   a. wait until the owner arrives
   b. drive away immediately
   c. leave a note with your name and address

3. What's an example of an "actual exhibit" you could bring as evidence to a small-claims trial?

   a. a coat ruined by a dry cleaner
   b. a witness to testify for you
   c. a written report

4. The 14th Amendment's guarantee of equal opportunity means that everyone must have what?

   a. the right to discriminate
   b. the same chance as everybody else
   c. a raise whenever they want one

GLOSSARY OF READING TERMS

adapted rewritten to be made shorter or easier to read

alliteration repetition of the initial sound in two or more words; a poetic device

analyze to identify and examine the separate parts of a whole

author's purpose the writer's specific goal or reason for writing a particular book, article, etc.

categorize to divide into main subjects or groups

cause a happening or situation that makes something else happen as a result

classify to organize according to some similarity

compare to make note of how two or more things are alike

compound word word made by combining two or more smaller words

conclusion the end or last part of a novel, article, etc.

context clues the words in a sentence just before and after an unfamiliar word or phrase. Context clues help to make clear what the unfamiliar word means.

contrast to make note of how two or more things are different from one another

describe to tell or write about something or someone in detail in order to help the reader or listener create a mental image

details bits of information or description that support the main idea and make it clearer

dialogue lines spoken by characters in a story or play

discuss to talk or write about a topic, giving various opinions and ideas

effect the reaction or impact that occurs as a result of a cause

elements the essential parts or components of a whole

excerpt section quoted from a book, article, etc.

fact something that actually happened or is really true

fiction literary work in which the plot and characters are imagined by the author

figurative language colorful, nonliteral use of words and phrases to achieve a dramatic effect

generalize to form a general rule or idea after considering particular facts

graphs charts or diagrams that visually present changes in something or the relationship between two or more changing things

homonyms words pronounced alike but having different meanings and usually different spellings

identify to name or point out; to distinguish someone or something from others

image idea, impression; a picture in the mind

inference conclusion arrived at by careful reasoning

interpret to explain the meaning of; to figure out in one's own way

judgment a decision made after weighing various facts

literature the entire body of written work including fiction, nonfiction, drama, poetry, etc.

locate find; tell where something is

main idea the point or central thought in a written work or part of a work

multiple-meaning words lookalike words that have different meanings in different contexts

nonfiction writing about the real world, real people, actual events, etc.

objective reflecting what is actual or real; expressed without bias or opinion

order items arranged or sequenced in a certain way, such as alphabetical order or order of importance

organize to put in place according to a system

outcome the result; the way that something turns out

parts of speech grammatical classifications of eight word types: adjective, adverb, conjunction, interjection, noun, preposition, pronoun, or verb

passage section of a written work

plot the chain of events in a story that leads to the story's outcome

plural word form showing more than one person, place, or thing

point of view the position from which something is observed or told; when a character tells the story, *first person* point of view is used; an author who tells the story in his own voice is using *third person* point of view.

predict to foretell what you think will happen in the future

prefix group of letters added at the beginning of a word to change the word's meaning or function

recall to remember or bring back to mind

refer to speak of something or call attention to it

relationship a connection of some kind between two or more persons, things, events, etc.

scan to glance at something or look over it quickly

sequence items in order; succession; one thing following another

singular word form naming just one person, place, or thing

subjective reflecting personal ideas, opinions, or experiences

suffix group of letters added at the end of a word that changes the word's meaning or function

symbol a concrete object used to represent an abstract idea

table an orderly, graphic arrangement of facts, figures, etc.

tense verb form that shows the time of the action, such as past, present, or future

term word or phrase with a special meaning in a certain field of study such as art, history, etc.

tone the feeling given by the author's choice of language

vocabulary all the words of a language